Lois Smith's

Machine Quiltmaking

Located in Paducah, Kentucky, the American Quilter's Society (AQS), is dedicated to promoting the accomplishments of today's quilters. Through its publications and events, AQS strives to honor today's quiltmakers and their work – and inspire future creativity and innovation in quiltmaking.

EXECUTIVE EDITOR: JANE R. MC CAULEY

BOOK DESIGN/ILLUSTRATIONS: LANETTE BALLARD

COVER DESIGN: KAREN CHILES

PHOTOGRAPHY: CHARLEY LYNCH

Library of Congress Cataloging-in-Publication Data

Smith, Lois Tornquist.
      Lois Smith's machine quiltmaking.
          p. 168   cm.
      Includes bibliographical references (p. 166).
      ISBN 0-89145-796-8
        1. Machine quilting.   2. Machine appliqué.   3. Patchwork quilts.
    I. Title.
    TT835.S55524   1997
    746.46--dc21   97-6202
                                                                   CIP

Additional copies of this book may be ordered from: American Quilter's Society, P.O. Box 3290, Paducah, KY 42002-3290 @ $19.95. Add $2.00 for postage & handling.

LET'S QUILT

CONTENTS

THE MAKING OF A QUILTMAKER

MAKING A SAMPLER QUILT

PLAYFUL ADDITIONS

The magic of quiltmaking unites generations producing a tangible expression of love and recorded history. Time modifies the vocabulary and the tools. The heart of quiltmaking remains.

Using acquired skills we move beyond tradition, expressing ourselves and our world in fabric, design, and color.

WORDS FROM THE AUTHOR...

When I first contemplated quiltmaking in the '70s, it was the historical connection that intrigued me. I liked the idea of trying my hand at an art enjoyed by previous generations. I romantically pictured pioneer children learning to quilt at their grandmother's knee.

My mother had been a skillful seamstress and rug braider. My aunts were always involved with sewing for the church bazaar. I was looking for my own creative niche. I wanted to be a quiltmaker!

My first try at quiltmaking had me so excited I could hardly sleep. I was anxious to run with this new experience. Rather than learn to quilt by hand, I started with the machine skills I had already learned. I was quickly on my way! Before I had even finished my first quilt, I was asked to teach quiltmaking by machine.

Most of the books available were for hand quiltmaking. Armed with a good technical background acquired while teaching sewing for S-T-R-E-T-C-H and SEW, I was able to translate the hand-quilting methods into machine quiltmaking skills. As I practiced, I kept notes. I refined and refined until I was satisfied that the machine methods were workable and technically correct. Though the tools were modernized, the traditional patterns remained as the foundation for my newly discovered passion.

The picture has changed. Now the grandmother teaching her granddaughter the joy of quiltmaking is me! (Yikes!) In time I hope she, and all who read this book, will come to love quiltmaking with a passion and will find the joy and satisfaction that comes with creating with your heart and soul.

Happy Stitching,

Lois Smith

BLOCK BY BLOCK

*You'll love the method!
You'll love the results!
You'll be so proud of
your finished quilt!*

*Use your sewing
machine to piece or
appliqué individual
quilt blocks which will
be quilted and
embellished before
being joined together
into a most magnificent
quilt.*

It's Fun!

It's Fantastic!

It's So Satisfying!

Prologue

Ready —

You have toyed with the thought of making a quilt for some time. Now is the time! *Machine Quiltmaking with Lois Smith* is your guidebook for the machine adventure of a lifetime.

Set —

The Making of a Quiltmaker. Is an introduction to the sewing machine and an overview of the tools and equipment needed.

Go!!

Making a Sampler Quilt presents detailed instructions for making a sampler quilt totally by machine. Each block will be pieced and quilted individually. There will be no bulky, hard-to-manage quilt to force through your machine. The eight lessons and their stipulated goals simulate a teaching situation. Skills and techniques are illustrated for easy understanding. Designs and templates for quilt block patterns are given in ascending order of difficulty.

A Gallery of Quilts

The gallery includes picture quilts based on traditional origins. You will see many of the blocks you are intending to make yourself presented in a variety of fabrics. The makers of the quilts will share with you their finished quilts in color. Fresh uses of traditional blocks will set your creative wheels in motion. You will read about the makers' personal successes. A prize-winning Southwestern quilt will be pictured along with instructions and patterns.

Playful Additions —

This section is devoted to having fun with color and textures. Simple fabric dyeing shortcuts will entice you. Surface design techniques will open up endless possibilities for adding texture to fabrics. Solve the mystery of working with metallic and other novelty threads. It's fun to play with fabrics and threads!

BLOCK DESIGNS

APPLIQUÉ BLOCKS

Assateague Lighthouse

Hearts and Flowers

CURVED DESIGNS

Clamshell

Drunkard's Path

Drunkard's Path Variations

Moon Over the Mountain

FIVE-PATCH BLOCKS

Cross and Crown

Flying Geese

Jack- in- the- Box

Red Cross

FOUR-PATCH BLOCKS

Anvil

Double Four Patch

Flock of Geese

God's Eye

King's X

Lightning

Pinwheel

Star Flower

Virginia Star

Wheels

Windblown Square

Yankee Puzzle

NINE-PATCH BLOCKS

Album

Bird of Paradise

Card Trick

54/40 or Fight

Maple Leaf

Ohio Star

Rail Fence

Spools

PICTURE BLOCKS

Airplane

Assateague Lighthouse

House on a Hill

Moon Over the Mountain

Roseville Bridge

Sailboat

SINGLE DESIGN BLOCKS

Crazy Patch or Time Capsule

Dresden Plate

Grandmother's Fan

Log Cabin and Log Cabin Variations

Strip Quilting

Strip Quilting Variations

INDIAN DESIGNS

Anvil

Arrowhead

Arrowheads

Ceremonial Face

A Gila Monster Named Jimmy

Hat Creek

Indian Star

Indian Trail

Kachina Dancer

Lightning

Squash Blossom

Teepee Village

Traditional Fish

Thunder and Lightning

Triplet

GETTING READY

Gather your tools and organize your space.

Check out quilting books in your local library. Start your own quilt book collection.

Cook in large quantities and freeze food for several meals. Simplify household tasks.

Join a local quilt group and look for a quilting buddy.

THE BASIC EIGHTY – A QUILTMAKER'S VOCABULARY

Alignment pin: a pin dropped in the seam lines of adjoining pieces to perfectly align fabric intersections before stitching.

alignment pin

Appliqué: shapes sewn to a foundation fabric creating a design or picture.

appliqué

Background: the visually receding or inconspicuous part of a block design.

background

Backing: fabric used for the back side of a quilt.

Backstitching: reverse stitching often used in garment construction at the beginning and end of seams to secure stitches. Not generally used in machine piecing.

Basting: the process of securing the three layers of a quilt together to prevent distortion during quilting.
- •Thread basting by hand: sewing long stitches by hand.
- •Pin basting: securing layers using small brass safety pins.
- •Tacking: inserting plastic tacks into the quilt using a special tool.

Batting: filler used in a quilt to give warmth and to add definition to the stitched designs. Cotton, polyester, or cotton/poly combinations are the most common types of batting. Wool and silk batting are also used.

Betweens: small, fine, needles, used in hand quilting.

(The) Betweens: author's term for sashing, horizontal strips of fabric cut the width of a block and used to join the blocks into vertical columns.

Block
Between
Block

Binding: narrow finishing strip on many quilts and wallhangings.

Blind hem stitch: a basic stitch found on most modern sewing machines. It can be used for invisible machine appliqué. The straight part of the stitches runs next to the appliqué on the background fabric. The "jump over" stitch catches and secures the appliqué. The blind hem foot is *not* used in this application.

Block: a completed design unit, usually in the form of a square, which is sewn to other blocks to complete the quilt top. Blocks may be pieced, appliquéd, or left plain for later quilting.

block

Block by block: construction technique which enables a block to be sandwiched with batting and backing and then quilted before being assembled into the quilt.

Blocking square: a grid drawn on an ironing board cover or fabric to facilitate accurate pressing.

blocking square

Borders: final or outside design rows of a quilt.

Chain piecing: assembly line piecing of fabrics without cutting thread between units.

chain piecing

Cheater cloth: printed fabric design that looks like a pieced or appliquéd quilt or quilt block.

Clean finish: the straight or crisp fabric edge created when the raw edge is trimmed away with a rotary cutter.

Color wheel: a graphic arrangement of the color spectrum.

color wheel

Cornerstones: small squares used at sashing intersections to add interest and to help align blocks.

cornerstones

Cutting mat: a self-healing mat, preferably marked with a grid, used in conjunction with the rotary cutter and a sturdy, plastic ruler.

cutting mat

Double stick tape: transparent tape with two tacky surfaces. Used on the bottom of plastic templates to secure the template to fabric for precise cutting.

Double needle: two or three needles on one shaft used for pin tucking and sewing multiple rows of parallel stitching at one time. Needles come in a variety of needle spacings as well as needle sizes. 4.0/100 indicates needles that are 4 mm apart with 100 size large needles.

double needle

Duckbill or appliqué scissors: sharp scissors with a duckbill shape blade. They are used for multilayered cutting of straight and curved pieces as well as for close trimming of appliquéd pieces.

Duckbill Scissors

Elastic thread: a stretchy thread which can be wound on the bobbin to create gathered or 3-D effects on fabric.

Embellishments: use of decorative threads, ribbons, beads, etc., to add interest and excitement to quilt surfaces.

Even feed foot: special sewing machine attachment which feeds the top and bottom layers of fabric evenly through the machine. Also called walking foot.

even feed foot

Feed dogs: the cleats or pads which advance the fabric automatically through the machine as stitches are formed.

Feed dogs dropped: feed dogs are inactivated by either being dropped into the machine bed or covered with a small plate attachment. This allows fabric to be moved manually for free-motion quilting.

feed dogs

Finished block size: refers to size of block after it is sewn into a quilt. A 12" block (finished size) will measure 12½" including seam allowances.

Fleece: a firm, needle-punched material good for place mats, wallhangings, and display walls.

Flexible curve: a flexible rubber bar used to draft curves and to mark sewing and cutting lines for some curved patchwork.

flexible curve

Food wrap: transparent paper for wrapping sandwiches. It is great as a stabilizer for machine stitching, pressing cloth substitute, and pattern paper for appliqué.

Foundation: muslin, lightweight fabric, or paper used as support for some types of piecing.

Free-motion stitching: machine quilting done by manually moving the fabric without the aid of feed dogs. A darning foot helps to protect fingers and to form quality stitches. Meander stitching is one form of free-motion stitching.

free motion stitching

Freezer paper: a food storage product used for pattern drafting, template making, and as an aid in appliqué. Shiny side will adhere to fabric when ironed.

Grain line: the direction of woven threads in a piece of fabric.

Bias: a line diagonal to the grain line in a fabric; stretchy; should be treated with care when used on edge of a piece to avoid distortion.

Crosswise grain: the alignment of fabric threads perpendicular to the selvage; has some stretch.

Lengthwise or straight of grain: the alignment of fabric threads parallel to the selvage, the tightly woven finished edges of the fabric; the lengthwise grain line has no stretch.

Invisible thread: a very fine monofilament thread used for quilting and appliqué which produces an almost invisible line of stitching.

Marking tools: pens or pencils used to place temporary quilting lines on fabric.
- •Vanishing pen: writes with a purple line and disappears by itself within 24 hours or less, depending on humidity levels.
- •Water Soluble Pen: writes with a blue line which may be removed with cold water.
- •Chalk: comes in a variety of forms:
  in container with serrated dispensing wheel
  as washout pencil
  in flat cake with a sharp edge
  in vanishing cake form
- •Silver pencil: marks dark fabrics and is easily removed by gentle rubbing with cloth.

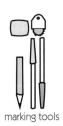

marking tools

Meander stitching: free-motion stitching where curves generally do not cross one another.

meandor stitching

Medallion: center design which is the main focus of a quilt. Borders surround center design and may echo its design elements. This type of quilt is called a Medallion quilt.

Miter: a seam with a 45° angle, commonly found in borders and binding.

miter

Nippers: a small scissorlike tool used for clipping threads.

Pieced: a quilt or block made up of geometric shapes sewn together.

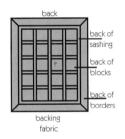
pieced

Points: sharp and complete ends of a pieced angle in a design. Star and triangle points should be complete and pointed, not blunted.

points

Point turner: a bluntly pointed tool for "poking out points" in appliqué.

point turner

Press: an up-and-down motion of the iron which produces a smooth surface but does not distort grain line. *Ironing* is a back-and-forth movement of the iron.

Quilt: two layers of fabric with an enclosed filler held together by stitching.

Quilt Parts:

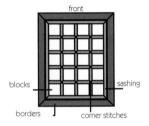

front / blocks / sashing / borders / corner stitches

back / back of sashing / back of blocks / back of borders / backing fabric

Reference point: marking on cut shapes to aid in proper alignment of pieces during piecing.

reference points

Regularly patterned fabric: yardage that is printed with a definite repeating design. Shapes should be aligned with pattern of fabric rather than grain line if straight alignment is desired.

wrong / right
regularly patterned fabric

Rotary cutter: cutting tool with a circular cutting blade for accurate and quick cutting of straight edges. Various sizes and styles are available.

rotary cutter

Sampler: a quilt intended to explore many different designs and sewing techniques.

Sashing: the joining strips of fabric that surround and unify the blocks. Also called stripping or lattice.

    (The) Betweens: horizontal sashing strips.

    Vertical Sashing: the strips that run from top to bottom of a quilt.

    Perimeter Sashing: outside rows of sashing enclosing quilt.

Sampler Quilt

Scrap quilt: a quilt made from many different fabrics, generally 50 or more. A scrap quilt can be made from new or collected fabrics.

Seam ripper: small tool with sharp, hooked end for removing stitches.

seam ripper

See through ruler: sturdy plastic ruler used with rotary cutter.

Selvage: tightly woven edges of yardage. Should be removed and not included in quilt piecing.

Shadow through: distracting seam allowance lines which are visible due to improper pressing or use of a fabric which is too thin or sheer. (Lining required.)

Speed piecing: techniques of assembly line piecing.

speed piecing

Stitch-in-the-ditch: stitching in the seam line.

Stripping: another name for sashing.

Surface texture: added stitching or manipulation of fabric to give dimension and interest to fabric.

surface texture center

Tagboard: lightweight cardboard sometimes used for templates.

Template: the pattern used for cutting a design piece.

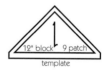
template

Template plastic: clear or frosted plastic used to make templates.

Ultra-Suede®: A suede-like fabric that works well for appliqué details since the edges do not fray and therefore do not need to be turned.

Unit: the basic mathematical division of a quilt block. There are four basic units in a Four-Patch, nine in a Nine-Patch, etc.

Value: the lightness or darkness of a color.

Viewing wall: display area where work in progress can be hung to be viewed and evaluated.

Viewing wall

Walking foot: same as even feed foot.

Whiskers: short, clipped ends of thread that protrude from quilt surface when not properly trimmed or hidden.

whiskers

Zinger: vibrant or unusual fabric which adds interest and energy to a quilt.

TOOLS AND EQUIPMENT NEEDED

BASIC EQUIPMENT

Sewing machine that has been cleaned, oiled, and adjusted
Chair that is comfortable and adjustable
Good lighting
Handy ironing surface with a 1" marked grid
Small iron
Spray water bottle

TOOLS

Large size rotary cutter (1¾" or 2⅜")
Self-healing cutting board (18" by 24" or larger)
Rulers: long, heavy duty plastic ruler, 24" or longer
    shorter, heavy duty plastic ruler, 12"
Quality 7" scissors for fabric
Inexpensive scissors for paper
Duckbill scissors (optional but very helpful)
Seam ripper

NOTIONS

Long, fine, glass-headed pins
Magnetic pincushion
Sewing thread, good quality cotton or polyester
Fabric marking tools
Freezer paper
12" vinyl floor tile
Color wheel

DRAFTING AND TEMPLATE EQUIPMENT

Graph paper (¼" grid), check for accuracy
Translucent, gridded tracing paper
Template materials: template plastic (regular), heat resistant template
    file folders or tag board
Pencils
Pencil sharpener
Double stick tape
Rubber Cement
Compass
Yardstick compass (optional)
Flexible curve (optional)

ORGANIZING AIDS

Notebook for storing notes and templates
Containers for quilt fabrics

I'M GOING TO MAKE A QUILT!

You have made the decision to become a quiltmaker. These tools are basic and important to your success. Collect them and keep them where you can find them. There are many tools available on the market; collect your basic tools first and then add others as you need them.

A PLACE FOR YOU

Claim some area of your home for your creative haven. Organize it till it meets your needs. Call it a studio, then produce works of art.

THE SEWING SPACE

Quiltmaking differs from garment sewing in that it is an ongoing process covering a longer period of time (possibly forever). Therefore, the closer you can get to a permanent sewing home, the better. Try to find yourself an area where you can wallow in scraps and ideas without offending others. I traded half of my laundry space to my husband for a large share of the basement. It was a good deal for both of us. Now I would like his remaining share of the basement, but I know better than to ask.

Whatever area you choose, organize it to suit your needs. This will take time, so be patient and creative. I found a supply of scrap carpet for my floor. I cut it into shapes and laid it in random quilt patterns. I like the warm feeling it gives and do not object to the fact that it needs to be vacuumed.

If unfinished projects start to pile up, store them along with the directions in a tote bag or basket out-of-sight but within easy finding distance. My sewing room fortunately has no ceiling, and I hang my baskets from the exposed rafters. A family member commented that I would pull the house down on myself if I was not careful. You do not need to be nagged by unfinished projects. Out-of-sight is out of mind for a while.

Control clutter by adding shelves and drawers. By keeping files of interesting projects or quilt blocks you would like to try, you will never let your creative well run dry. Store these ideas in a notebook or filing cabinet. Filing cabinets not only can keep you organized, but may also be used to support your cutting table if they are the proper height.

IMPORTANT: Work toward installing a viewing wall where work in progress can be displayed. Extruded polystyrene insulation board, which comes in ½" or ¾" thicknesses, works great. It is lightweight, easy to cut to size, and can be installed simply by covering with flannel and pushing into place. The flannel will grip most small fabric pieces. Larger pieces in progress may need a pin or two.

WORK CENTER

These areas save time and frustration and improve organization of your sewing area.

CUTTING CENTER

cutting board (They come in sizes large enough to cover your whole tabletop.)

rotary cutter

rulers

scissors

double stick tape

pencils

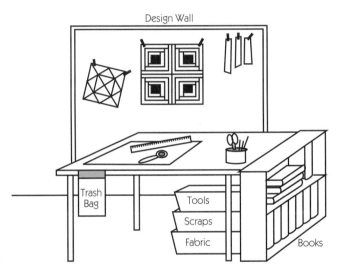

LIBRARY

Arrange books alphabetically.

Keep a written record of your books to avoid duplicate purchases.

Record information on any loaned books.

SEWING CENTER

machine(s) with accessories

thread caddy nearby

good lighting

small scissors

seam ripper

small ruler

PRESSING AREA ADJACENT TO SEWING AREA

small iron

spray water bottle

1" gridded ironing surface

SEWING CENTER

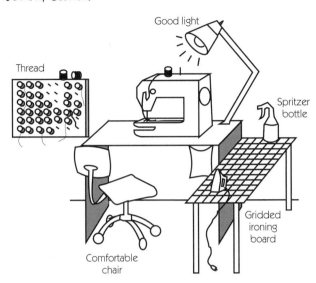

DRAFTING AREA

If you have room for a separate drafting area, great; if you do not, try to keep all drafting tools together:

> graph paper
>
> pencils
>
> pencil sharpener
>
> ruler
>
> template plastic
>
> rubber cement
>
> paper scissors
>
> compass
>
> yardstick compass (optional)
>
> flexible curve (optional)
>
> T-square

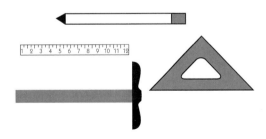

In addition to the necessities, add the things that will make your sewing time even more enjoyable such as a telephone, radio, CD player, and possibly a TV.

THE MAKING OF A QUILTMAKER

FEATURES IMPORTANT TO QUILTMAKERS:

- Snap on and off machine feet
- Good straight stitch formation
- Satin stitch that is smooth and well-packed
- Variable stitch width (zigzag) capability as opposed to only preset small, medium, and wide options
- Changeable needle positions
- Feed dog drop capability
- Darning foot for free-motion stitching
- Built-in even feed foot
- Knee lifter for lifting presser foot
- Decorative stitches that you like
- Controls that allow easy changing of stitches
- Availability of additional machine feet

No one machine has all the features, so choose the features that are important to you.

THE SEWING MACHINE

Quilts can be beautifully pieced on any well-tuned sewing machine that produces a good, secure straight stitch. Older machines may lack the useful blind hem or zigzag capability that is frequently used for appliqué, but this deficiency can be overcome quite well by substituting a straight stitch. While the stitch on the older basic machine may be acceptable, the foot pedal that controls the speed of the stitching may be a problem when attempting free-motion quilting. A speedy or jerky stitching rhythm makes producing a smooth and flowing design a challenge, but not an impossibility. Newer machines generally have a variety of speeds possible with slight changes in foot pressure. This is an advantage for piecing as well as quilting.

It is a good idea to talk with other quilters about their machines and to determine just what features you need. A used brand name machine is often a better investment than a discount store model. Demonstrator classroom models at quilt shows and sewing machine stores are a good value. You should allow yourself some room for growth in a machine, but do not spend money on features you know you will never use. Contrary to popular belief, buying the top of the line machine is not always the best idea.

UNDERSTANDING AND CARING FOR YOUR MACHINE

Your sewing machine is an important part of a beautiful quilt. The more you know and understand your machine, the better you can react to it. Giving your machine a pet name is fine, but do more than that. Read your sewing machine manual several times. Consult your machine dealer when questions arise that you cannot answer. Maintain your machine in smooth working order by proper cleaning and lubrication with quality sewing machine oil. Since many machines need frequent oiling, learn where to oil your machine. Oil reduces the friction on moving parts and keeps the machine running smoothly and quietly. Lubricate after long periods of sewing, but avoid oiling too often. If you have used too much oil, put a little alcohol on a lint free cloth or cotton swab and clean the inside of the machine. Then oil the movable parts with sewing machine oil before running the motor again.

By keeping a small brush handy you will be able to whisk out loose threads and lint from around the bobbin and feed dog areas every time you change your bobbin. A small vacuum attachment is available as a dust and lint remover for computers and sewing machines. This is a great tool and far preferable to blowing the lint into the machine with a hair drier or compressed air. My dealer also suggests a light application of silicone lubricant applied inside the bobbin case with a cotton swab to reduce friction.

An annual professional cleaning and oiling is recommended for all machines. Your sewing machine dealer probably has a recommended mechanic. Be a little fussy in choosing your machine's mechanic, and ask for a maintenance report.

YOUR MACHINE NEEDS TO BE READY FOR QUILTMAKING

Verify threading and bobbin insertion with the owner's manual. (It does make a difference!)
Establish a method for stitching a ¼" seam.
Using a piece of ¼" grid graph paper, check the distance from the needle (dropped on a line) to the right side of the presser foot. It should be ¼". If not:

- adjust needle position, if possible
- search accessories box for a ¼" presser foot
- purchase a ¼" presser foot

Check tension and stitch appearance on fabric/batting sample:

- Stitches should be even and secure on top and back of fabric.
- Rows of stitching should be smooth to the touch.

The tension on the thread is controlled by the tension regulator — a dial, knob, or digital display screen on the front of every machine. It is generally numbered from zero to ten — zero being no tension, ten being the tightest. An adjustment to the tension on the thread is made by changing the tension regulator slightly. A turn to the right or larger number tightens the top tension. A turn to the left, smaller numbers, loosens the tension. There are times when it may become necessary to loosen the top tension slightly:

- when using a lighter weight thread such as invisible nylon thread in the needle with a heavier weight bobbin thread
- when the bobbin thread is showing on the top of the quilt surface
- when the top thread starts to break frequently

Many of us have been taught *"Never, Never touch the tension on the bobbin case!"* A factory-set bobbin case should give you a good tension for normal sewing for quite a while. After time, however, it can get out of perfect working order, and you can remedy it yourself. In machines with removable bobbin cases, the bobbin thread should support the bobbin case in air when held by the extending thread. A slight jerk on the thread should cause the bobbin case to drop slightly.

- adjust loose tension by turning screw to right
- adjust too tight tension by turning screw to left

If you like to experiment with various thread and effects caused by purposely changing the thread and bobbin tensions, then it is a good idea to buy an extra bobbin case which you can adjust. Put a fingernail polish mark on it to identify it.

HINT

If the back of the fabric indicates a tension problem, it is generally caused by the top tension. Thread the top thread again, making sure the presser foot is in the raised position while threading.

- Loops on the back (spaghetti) suggest that the presser foot was not lowered during stitching. Lower presser foot.
- Thread laying flat on the back suggests loose top tension.

Sometime experimentation overrides reason!
A poor tension evident on the top of the fabric generally indicates a tension problem in the bobbin. Check to see that the thread is correctly engaged in the bobbin case tension disk.

- Check bobbin case tension and make adjustment.

SEWING MACHINE NEEDLES

All sewing machine needles may break, become dull, or acquire burrs. This applies to double needles and specialty needles as well your everyday needles. Sewing machine needles need to be replaced after approximately eight hours of sewing. Keep a variety of sizes on hand. Needles have points which range from ballpoint to very sharp. Each type of needle is designed to perform a different sewing task. Universal or sharp work well for piecing and quilting. When exchanging one needle for another, run your fingers down the needle to check for any burrs or rough spots near or around the point. Discard if any are found.

Some of the Schmetz needles are color coded to help you choose the proper needle for the job.

•Universal Needles H: This multi-purpose needle comes in a large range of sizes from very fine 8/60 to a very sturdy 19/120. The eye is small and appropriate for fine to medium weight threads. The larger size has a larger eye, but the bulk of the needle makes it difficult to stitch through many layers. The needle point is slightly blunted and may produce straight stitches that appear to angle.

•The Denim/Jeans Needle H-J: The sharp point of this needle allows it to penetrate fabrics easily. Sizes 10/70 and 12/80 are great for piecing and stitching in the ditch. Size 10/70 is quite fragile, so take care if sewing over pins. Needle sizes range from 10/70 to 18/110. The smaller sizes are fairly new on the market.

•The Quilting Needle H-Q (green shank): This needle has a special taper to the point along with a deeper grove and elongated eye to help delicate rayon and other fine quilting threads pass through the fabric and batting without fraying and breaking.

•Embroidery Needle (red dot on rounded base): This needle is designed with a larger eye, a grove profile to handle metallic and other heavy and irregular decorative threads, and a point which is blunted slightly to avoid damaging the thread. The 11/75 works well with metallics, the 14/90 can sew some of the heavier threads. These needles make it possible to try thread not previously considered suitable for machine stitching.

•Top Stitching Needle N: This is the original sharp-pointed needle with an enlarged eye. It helps to produce straight stitches and it also works well with metallics and heavier threads. Available in

sizes 12/80/, 14/90, and 16/100.

•Metallica Needle: This needle has an elongated eye made to accommodate metallic threads.

•Metafil Needle (Beka): This needle has a slightly larger eye which is coated with a teflon-like substance to help metallic and novelty threads slip through the needle without breaking.

When purchasing sewing machine needles, buy them in a variety of sizes and styles. For best results use the smallest size needle that will do the job successfully. A needle that is too large may leave holes in the fabric.

BASIC THREADS

Thread used for piecing may be polyester, cotton, or cotton/polyester. It should be high quality with long, staple fibers which give it a smooth appearance. If thread appears to be fuzzy, it will leave lint inside your machine. Discard any thread that is old and fuzzy.

Quilting thread can be anything that adds interest to your piece as long as it will fit through the machine needle. Rayon and acrylic threads add sheen to the quilt surface. Metallic thread adds an unexpected sparkle. Thread marked "Hand Quilting Thread" is generally waxed and meant for hand quilting only. The resin on it is not good for the machine.

Invisible nylon is a monofilament thread which looks much like a soft fishing line but is as fine (.004mm) as hair. It comes in a smoke color to blend with most colors or a clear to use with pastels. It is used most frequently for invisible stitching in the seam line and for invisible appliqué. Decorative threads come in a wide variety of weights and textures. See section three for instructions on use.

THE ROTARY CUTTER

The rotary cutter is not a gimmick. It will never totally replace a good pair of scissors, but it is an important tool for quilters today. The rotary cutter has revolutionized straight line cutting, making strip cutting faster and more accurate. This circular cutting tool is used with a cutting mat and a long, sturdy ruler.

Rotary cutters come in a variety of sizes and styles. All have a security guard to help prevent accidental cuts when the rotary cutter is resting. One type has a security blade guard that must be manually locked in place. This type is the best for you if you have young children. Another brand has a guard that slips out-of-the-way with the gentle pressure exerted when cutting. This one is fine in an adult sewing room. There are also handles designed for those with orthopedic concerns. Rotary cutter blade sizes vary from 1" diameter to 2⅜". The larger the blade, the faster the cutting job.

When you purchase a cutter, it is a good idea to buy at least one extra blade to have in reserve. Blades get nicked by coming in contact with a pin or other hard object left in the cutting path. The result is an annoying skip in the cut which requires another run with the rotary cutter or little snips with scissors. This cut repair can be very bothersome and time consuming. The moral of this story is, "keep foreign objects off the cutting surface!" If I get a nick in a blade that has been used for six months, I don't hesitate to replace it. A nick in a new blade, however, brings forth feelings of irritation and the need to be frugal. Forget it! Put in a new blade and keep that cutting surface clean. It is not a bad idea to have two rotary cutters. The one with the newer blade can be reserved for fabric, while the duller one can be used to cut paper and other straight edges.

CUTTING MATS

Rotary cutting mats come in a variety of styles and sizes. Most are marked with a 1" grid to aid in cutting straight lines. Small sizes are available for travel and taking to workshops. One style has an ironing pad on the reverse side and is a delight to have next to your sewing machine.

Practical mat sizes for sewing rooms range from 18" x 24" up to 32" x 60". The size of your cutting space will determine what size will work best for you. A space saver table in also available with drop sides that pull up to accommodate a large cutting mat which can be rolled and stored underneath when not in use. This table is a little higher than your average table and is a good back saver. Cutting mats are self-healing and will last for years as long as they are kept flat or stored flat or loosely rolled. A word of warning, however. Do not buy a cutting mat during a heat wave. Just carrying mine from the store to the car in 100° heat permanently warped one side.

CUTTER, MAT & RULER

A DYNAMIC TRIO FOR QUILTMAKERS

Always practice safety — replace security guard on cutter whenever it is not in use.

Place a sticker or masking tape date on your cutter each time you change the blade.

RULERS

Rulers complete the rotary cutting trio. Several 24" rulers are on the market, each with its own advantages. One has a lip that hooks over the edge of the cutting mat and acts like a T-square to keep the ruler from slipping during cutting. Another has special ridges on the bottom to prevent it from slipping. A third is double printed in yellow and black so lines can be seen on any color fabric. All of them are good. In time you may want to purchase more than one.

In addition a plastic 6" or 12" ruler is helpful in cutting individual shapes using templates. The ruler is placed over the template and protects the template edge during cutting.

GRAIN LINE CONSIDERATIONS

Although you will be cutting layers of fabric at one time, the position of the grain line in the fabric is still important and not to be ignored.

In the manufacturing process the fabric is often pressed or stretched on the bolt so that the cross grain and the lengthwise grain are not exactly perpendicular.

By washing and pressing by hand or with an iron, fabric can be straightened somewhat. However, you may end up with one of these two situations:

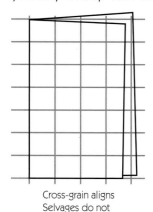
Cross-grain aligns
Selvages do not

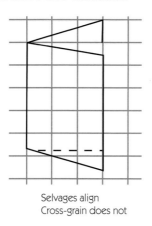
Selvages align
Cross-grain does not

Since the fabrics in my area are torn across the grain line at the time of purchase, I align the cross grain and cut from there.

If your fabrics were rotary cut at the time of purchase, align the selvage.

When working with solid color fabric where the grain lines are noticeable, cut a single layer of fabric at a time to keep the grain line visually pleasing.

CUTTING

The rotary cutter looks and performs like a pizza cutter. By rolling the cutter along the ruler's edge, two or more layers of folded fabric will be cut into strips. These strips may be used as strips or recut into smaller pieces later.

For a right-handed person, the aligned edges of the fabric will be coming from the right side to the left, the fold of the fabric nearest your body.

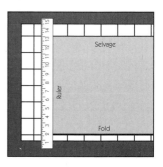

A left-handed person will work with the fabric coming from the left-hand side, fabric fold closest to the body. To achieve an accurate measurement,

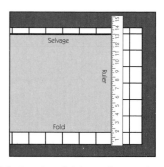

the raw edge of the fabric should be trimmed or given a clean finish.

To clean finish the edge:
- Place fold of fabric on a grid line.
- Barely cover edge of fabric with ruler.
- Align ruler with grid line on mat.
- Cut off raw or uneven fabric edge.

To cut:
- Position flat side of the wheel against the ruler.
- Place index finger on handle on top of cutter.
- Use downward pressure on the wheel.
- Move cutter along ruler away from your body.

THE SAMPLER QUILT

A SAMPLER QUILT is an introduction to the realm of quiltmaking; it is the quilter's liberal arts education! In this book a variety of blocks representing different categories and techniques are explored. The categories include pieced, appliqué, strip pieced, crazy patch, and Log Cabin.

Accuracy in cutting and piecing will become obvious immediately because the blocks made must be completed to the same size even though a variety of patterns and techniques are used. This precision will become natural and actually enjoyable.

Your uniqueness as an individual will become apparent as you choose fabrics and designs and put them together in a manner that pleases you. By the time you have completed a sampler quilt, you will be a skilled and accomplished quiltmaker.

Start at the beginning: learn the basics. Create a sampler quilt as you acquire new skills and techniques. Soar into the wonderful world of quiltmaking. Get started! Your enthusiasm will carry you to the finish.

EIGHT LESSONS

This section of the book is divided into eight lessons. Each is similar to a classroom teaching session in which various skills and goals are presented and accomplished. Completing the quilt blocks is the homework. A lesson can realistically be completed in two to four weeks. The goal of the eight lessons...*to finish* a sampler quilt!

Suggestions and patterns are given for making 12" blocks. The progression increases skill level from one block to the next. Each new block presents a slightly different challenge in color choices as well as technique.

MINI-SUCCESSES AND THEN...THE THRILL OF A FINISHED QUILT!

Block-by-block construction will be used in making the sampler. The finished blocks will be layered with both batting and backing and then machine quilted before the sashing is added and the blocks are joined together. Since each layered block will be only about 12" square, you will have the freedom to machine quilt without the bulk or drag of a full quilt. The entire process can be done beautifully on the machine, if you choose.

PLANNING

A sampler is unique in that it takes little advanced design planning other than choosing colors and perhaps a theme. There is no need to draw a specific layout. You can jump in with both feet and get started. If your initial fabric selections work well together, your quilt blocks will be great. If you need additional fabric as you progress, just add them. To assure a pleasant balance of color and design, the final arrangement of the blocks will be done after the squares have been completed.

GATHERING FABRICS

The quilt begins and gets its impact from the fabrics you choose. Using these fabrics as you desire will make your quilt unique and lovely.

SELECTING FABRICS

A sampler quilt can accommodate a variety of fabrics. My sampler quilts generally have only two or three color families but 50 different fabrics. Depth and interest come from having a good color scheme that is well executed. While you are learning the fundamentals of machine quiltmaking, you are also having fun placing fabrics next to one another and discovering relationships of color and value.

As you start selecting fabrics, note the manufacturer's name. You will be more satisfied with top quality fabrics in your blocks. Be an educated consumer.

Many fabric manufacturers currently employ quilters as design advisors. Bright contemporary fabrics are available as well as "repro" fabrics. These are reproductions of fabrics typical of early periods in history. You can purchase fabrics from the Civil War era, Victorian period, light pastel fabrics from the 1930s, or hand-dyed fabrics and batiks.

Patronize the shops that specialize in quilt-related fabrics and items. It is there that you will get quality fabrics and the help that you need from knowledgeable salespeople. Quilt shops appreciate your business and the salespeople will enjoy following your progress.

CHOOSE A KEY FABRIC

Your first trip to the fabric store can be overwhelm-

ing. However, try to focus on finding one spectacular, multicolored fabric which will be your key fabric. Walk around without seeking help until you find a bolt that knocks your socks off!

VISUALIZE THE EFFECT YOU WANT

Before choosing the others, visualize a quilt built around this particular fabric. Take another step and relate your quilt to something in your experience. Does it give the feel of a Monet garden or perhaps wildflowers in bloom? Have you chosen a fabric of the 30s or a jungle print with animals? Maybe this quilt will be the remembrance of a vacation to the seashore, the mountains, or the backwoods. Let your imagination run free.

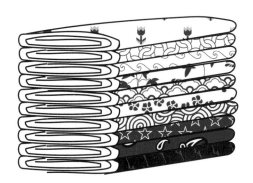

CHOOSE FABRICS CAREFULLY

Select fabrics in a wide variety of prints (small, medium, and large scale) and a wide range of color values (light, medium, dark, and extra dark). Fabrics do not have to match each other, but all of them should blend or relate to the key selection. Stack the bolts of fabrics, graduating the color values from dark to light. Take a good look at the combined fabrics. If there are big gaps in the value range, add more bolts. At this point you are looking for a gradual blending from light to dark that is personally pleasing. Look for a smooth flow of color and value.

If you can't find all the fabrics you are looking for at one shop, get what you can and fill in with others as you go along. You do not need to buy everything at one time, but it does help to have your swatches with you as you shop.

FABRIC REQUIREMENTS

Bed size	No. of Blocks	Fabric for blocks	Backing fabric	Border fabric
Twin	20	7½ yds. assrt. fabrics	7½ yds.	3½ yds. (opt)
Double/Queen	20	7½ yds. assrt. fabrics	11 yds.	3½ yds.
King	25	8½ yds. assrt. fabrics	12 yds.	3½ yds.

Although it is too early to completely visualize your quilt, chances are that your key fabric will be a good border choice or become part of the border. It will unify your quilt. This fabric, however, will probably not be around in the store when you are at the finishing stages of your quilt. Suggestion: buy an extra 3½ yards of the key fabric. Put it away with the hope that you will use it later. If it doesn't work out, it can be the start of another quilt project.

Batting: There is some waste in cutting and in the use of block-by-block construction techniques. Buy a little more than the desired finished quilt size. Please see appendix for complete bed and yardage charts.

SELECT

One yard of the multicolored *key fabric*.
Also purchase 3½ yds. more if you plan to use this fabric in the border.
- Prints which coordinate with key fabric:
   a. Small allover print (½ yd.)
   b. Medium size print (½ yd.)
   c. Large, widely spaced print (½ yd.)
   d. Large allover print (½ yd.)
- Prints with different color values:
   a. Light color fabric (½ yd.)
   b. Medium color fabric (½ yd.)
   c. Dark color fabric (½ yd.)
   d. Extra dark color fabric (½ yd.)
- One or two solid or almost solid fabrics (½ yd. of each)
- One or two light, small print, or swirl pattern for background (¾ yd. of each)
- Zinger fabric for accent (¼ yd.)

BACKING, SASHING, AND BATTING

BACKING

The backing fabric should coordinate with the top fabrics. An allover print in the medium value range is excellent. It allows for inconspicuous changes in the bobbin thread color, if necessary, and also camouflages minor thread tension problems.

Stripes and plaids should be avoided since the back will be cut into block-size working sections, and matching the design line would impossible.

Though solid colors do not present design problems, quilting flaws are more visible than on a print fabric. Also, any shading variations due to grain line position of the block in the quilt will be obvious.

SASHING OR STRIPPING

The sashing will be selected later after the majority of blocks have been completed. The sashing fabric is extremely important in completing the feel and balance of the total picture. Please wait to buy this fabric until your blocks have started to show their personality. See the appendix for yardages.

BATTING

Batting comes in three lofts or weights: high, medium, and low loft. Cotton, polyester, and cotton/poly are common quilt batts. Wool and silk are specialty fillers.

High loft is recommended for comforters and quilts which are to be tied. It is not generally recommended for machine quilting by the block as the extra loft has a tendency to distort the design when quilted.

Low loft is recommended for use in clothing and miniature quilts and in places where you want a very lightweight quilt. Since machine quilting has a tendency to compress a block somewhat, low loft batting will create a quilt that is very flat.

Regular loft batting works well in a quilt that is to be machine quilted block by block. Cotton or polyester batt is fine. Polyester batt is excellent for quilts that will be washed frequently as it will not disintegrate inside the quilt. Look at the samples of batting and choose one that appears to cling to the fabric without sliding. Read the package. Does it have to be prewashed? How close does it need to be quilted? Do not select one that requires quilting every 2" or closer.

The regular loft polyester batting allows quilting definition without pucker. The cut edges of the batting can generally be pulled slightly or "feathered" to make joining to the sashing smooth and without bulk.

Cotton batting relates to the history of quiltmaking. It does not have as much loft as polyester batt, but many prefer this antique or flatter look.

WASH FABRICS

Since the quilt that you are making will probably be washed sometime, it is a good idea to prewash all fabrics to reduce the risk of future uneven shrinkage and to get rid of excess dye and other chemicals that might run and stain your finished quilt. Cotton fabrics shrink an average of 1" per yard. Muslin and other loosely woven fabrics can shrink as much as 3" per yard.

Often fabrics will bleed, especially red, brown, and highly saturated ones. There is a product on the market available at most quilt stores that is a prewash solution which stops bleeding. By following the directions on the bottle and watching the rinse water to make sure that it is clear, you can use these fabrics with confidence.

HINT
Fabric Swatch Record

Adding fabrics to your quilt will be a continuous pleasure. Carrying swatches from your quilt fabrics will make you more successful at selecting additional fabrics. Slip a small piece of each original fabric on a safety pin or glue small swatches to a 3" x 5" card to carry in your purse or wallet.

T here are many skills to be considered and learned in the process of making a quilt. By working step-by-step through the following lessons, you will soon feel confident and accomplished.

FOUR-PATCH BLOCKS

Pieced blocks will be constructed in several of the lessons. In Lesson One you will be working with the Four-Patch designs using templates.

MAKING TEMPLATES

•

CUTTING FABRICS

•

PIECING

•

PRESSING

•

STANDARDS

GOALS OF LESSON ONE

•Learn to recognize Four-Patch blocks
•Make five different Four-Patch blocks

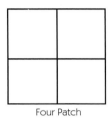
Four Patch

SKILLS

•Recognizing Four-Patch designs
•Template making
•Making fabric choices
•Cutting techniques
  Grain line awareness
  Pieces from strips
•Piecing techniques
  Machine settings
  Chain sewing
•Pressing techniques

DESIGN CATEGORIES

Before a design can be re-created in fabric, the organization of the block design must be recognized.

The Double Four-Patch block is made up of four equally-sized sections. All four sections of the block are the same size even though two sections are made up of only one square, and the other two each have four smaller squares.

When the block category is determined, the block can be divided into units. The 12" Four-Patch design has a basic unit of 6". Each 6" unit can be subdivided into different shapes.

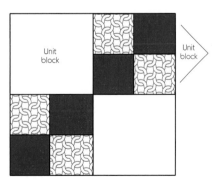
Unit block

Unit block

Double Four-Patch

In this lesson you will be using templates which are patterns for the shapes you will be joining. In subsequent lessons you will also be introduced to alternative methods of cutting without templates.

TEMPLATES

The templates that you will be making in this lesson will be of durable plastic and will be used to make the first five blocks of your quilt. Then these templates will be stored for later use.

One 6" unit block template will be made, and other templates will be constructed from subdivisions of a unit block. These shapes will be isolated and a ¼" seam allowance will be added to each one.

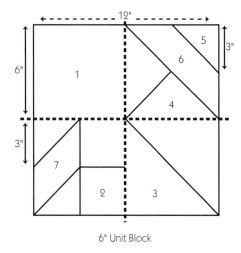

6" Unit Block

MAKING TEMPLATES

Accurate templates are used to cut the fabric into the correct shape. By learning to draft your own templates, you will extend your quiltmaking knowledge and flexibility. You will be able to draft and construct almost any design that you see, no matter what the size. Drafting skills are worth the little time and effort necessary to acquire them.

Templates are, however, included with each section of this book. You may carefully trace these patterns on graph paper and glue them to template plastic.

GRAPH PAPER

There are several different qualities of ¼" grid graph paper available for making templates. One is available in the grocery or drugstore and is generally accurate and inexpensive. Another type can be

found in an art supply store. It is transparent and more expensive, but works well for drafting and tracing templates out of a book.

The 12 blocks in this Four-Patch category can be made with the following seven shaded shapes (say that seven times!) made into templates.

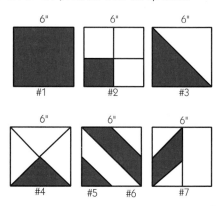

TEMPLATE DRAFTING

- •Draw the basic unit blocks on graph paper.
- •Divide and isolate the shapes as indicated in the above diagram.
- •Add ¼" seam allowances on all sides of the shapes.
- •Make a rough cut of each shape, and glue it to template plastic with rubber cement.
- •When the cement has dried, cut out the template.
- •Mark grain line.
- •Label: 12" block, Four-Patch, date, and your initials.
- •Check size for accuracy against the templates in the book.

Please also note: The extending points of the seam allowance should be blunted, leaving only the ¼" seam allowance above or beyond the tip of the original triangle. This makes matching of the joining sides easier and more accurate.

> **HINT**
>
> Graph paper markings should not be used to add the ¼" seam allowances to the diagonal sides of a triangle. Use the ¼" guideline on your plastic ruler.

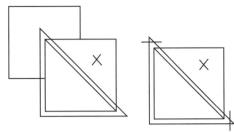

MAKING INITIAL FABRIC CHOICES

One of the fascinations of quiltmaking is the fun of working with color and design. The planning of a block involves putting one fabric with another. Colors must be placed to look attractive together and to present the design of the block to its best advantage.

Most often a quilt block is composed of two elements: a design and a background. The design is meant to capture the attention of the viewer. The background is meant to be low key and not compete for attention. A contrast in value between the design and the background is vital to the success of a design.

After successfully choosing the fabric combinations for one block, you can use this combination again for the starting point of the next block. By just making one or two substitutions you will have another fabric grouping.

The 12 blocks in this section are shown in fabrics. This will give you a clue as to value and scale placement; however, make any alterations you choose. These fabric choices are only suggestions.

HINT
Remember each time you select fabrics for a block:
light, medium, dark: (values)
small, medium, large: (prints)

CUTTING AND GRAIN LINES

Careful attention to cutting makes a visually pleasing block. Using the rotary cutter and a template to cut shapes from a cut strip of fabric produces excellent results quickly and easily. (Please review the Rotary Cutting section, if necessary.)

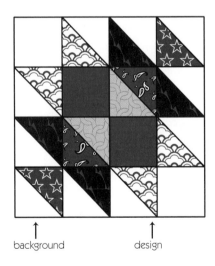

background   design

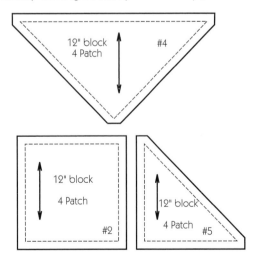

When measuring the templates for the Four-Patch, you will note the depth measurement of the template is either 6½" or 3½". After deciding on your fabrics, cut one strip of each the appropriate depth of the template times the width of the fabric. If you have marked the grain line on your template, you should have no trouble aligning the template with the grain line in the fabric and cutting your shapes.

VARIETY, VALUE, SCALE

With every block you make, you will go through the same process of first selecting the design and then choosing the fabrics. Three words will help: variety, value, and scale. Your block should have a range of fabrics which go from light to dark (value), and the scale of the prints should be varied (small, medium, and large).

Place double stick tape on the very edge of the plastic side of the template.

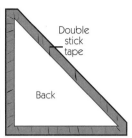

Place the template on the fabric strip, sticky side down.

Protect the template with a plastic ruler as you cut with a rotary cutter.

HINT

As a double check, align the ¼" guideline on a ruler with the original line on the template (before seam allowance is added). This is especially helpful when templates get older and may have accidentally been shaved off a bit on the edges.

ADVANTAGES OF CUTTING FROM A STRIP

- Working with small piece of fabric is comfortable.
- Results are accurate.
- Color combinations are easier to visualize with small fabric pieces.
- Several layers can be cut simultaneously.
- Room clutter is reduced.

Stripes, plaids, and fabrics with a regularly spaced

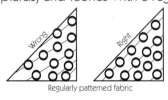

Regularly patterned fabric

design should be cut individually to assure a pleasing visual outcome regardless of grain line. With double stick tape on the template, fabric shapes can be accurately cut with rotary cutter or scissors.

THE GOLDEN RULE OF GRAIN LINE

 Whenever possible and practical, avoid the use of bias grain line on the outside edges of a block.

CREATIVE GRAIN LINE CUTTING

A straight edge will stabilize a bias seam. When two long bias seams are to be sewn together, it may be attractive and desirable to cut the longest piece straight of grain. This will give you a small section of bias on the outside edge, so take care not to stretch this area. (See Wheels and Wind-blown Square in the block section.)

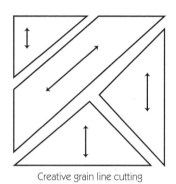

Creative grain line cutting

STANDARDS OF GOOD WORKMANSHIP (CUTTING)

- Pieces should be cut accurately and consistently placed in relation to the fabric grain line.
- Regularly patterned fabric should be cut in relation to the pattern of the fabric to avoid the illusion of inaccuracy.

POSITIONING FLEECE

As the pieces are cut, they should be placed in the design position so they will soon be ready to sew together. Polyester fleece works well for this. Polyester fleece is a sturdy, needle-punched, thin batting that is excellent for temporarily positioning cut design pieces.

The fleece has almost a magnetic attraction which holds the pieces securely until needed. The design can even be hung on a wall for viewing from a different angle.

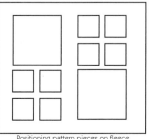

Positioning pattern pieces on fleece

A 15" by 15" square will allow plenty of room for laying out the design. Have several squares cut and handy. Some days creative color combinations just seem to flow. Use this energy to cut several blocks and position them on the fleece for piecing later.

Before sewing the pieces together, take time to evaluate your design and fabric choices. Is this what you had in mind? Do you suddenly have a better idea? Don't be afraid to make substitutions and recut a piece or two. I have been known to redo practically the whole block until I am satisfied with my choices. Save any unused pieces. Chances are that they will get a second chance to be used before the quilt is finished.

MACHINE PIECING

Piecing is the sewing together of small pieces to make units. These are generally sewn into rows, and the rows are joined into a finished block.

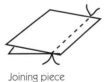

Join the smallest pieces first; place right sides of the fabric facing each other, right sides together. Sew with a ¼" seam allowance.

Joining piece

Set your machine at #2 stitch length which is about 14 stitches an inch. This tight stitch will be secure and thread will not be visible in the seam line.

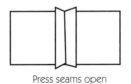

Stitch from the edge of the fabric to the opposite edge; do not backstitch. Press seams open.

Press seams open

Machine stitched seams are very strong and are not weakened by being pressed open. An open seam has less bulk when it is joined to like pieces and makes the intersecting seam line easier to align.

POINTS TO REMEMBER

• The distance from the needle to the right side of the presser foot must be ¼", as this is the amount of seam allowance you added to the template.

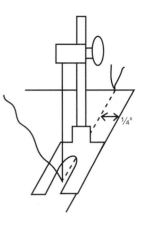

• Backstitching is intended to lock beginning and ending stitches. When piecing with 14 stitches per inch, the tight stitch prevents stitches from pulling out. Backstitching is unnecessary.

• When four or more seams come together at an intersection, the seam lines should be aligned.

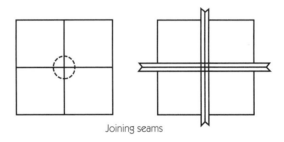

Joining seams

To refine the alignment, press a straight pin vertically through both seams of joining pieces, ¼" from the raw edge. Turn the pieces over to make sure that the

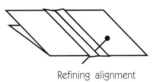

Refining alignment

pin is also in the seam line on the underside. If not, make a slight adjustment. Pin again and then sew.

Understand the standards of good workmanship, but set your own goals. Every quiltmaker has times when points get blunted accidentally or something is less than perfect. Quiltmaking should be fun! Always work to perfect your skills, but don't let perfection spoil your quiltmaking enjoyment!

STEP BY STEP...THE DOUBLE FOUR PATCH

• Select appropriate templates: use template #1 and #2. (Learn to see the templates as fractions of the unit square.)

• Choose the fabrics. Blocks require a pleasing variety in value (light and dark) and in print size and spacing.

• Cut shapes.

• Lay out total block.

• Join smallest pieces first.

• Press seams open.

• Sew into units, matching seam lines.

• Press seams open.

• Join units into rows.

• Join rows into block.

• Make intersecting seams match perfectly.

• Press carefully again.

Measure block. It should be 12½" on each side. (12" plus two ¼" seam allowances.)

You have finished your first quilt block.

CHECK POINT: BLOCK SIZE

If your first block is not 12½" from edge to edge, stop now! Are your templates correct? Did you cut carefully? Is your ¼" seam allowance accurate? Learn to be your own troubleshooter!

When each block has been finished, place it on your viewing wall. Seeing the fabric combinations from a distance gives a new perspective. Each completed block will help make future fabric choices. Continue with a successful color combination, making substitutions in pattern or in color. Learn from your experience.

> *It only takes a little more effort do it right! Your seam ripper is your friend!*

FLOCK OF GEESE

This block is always an eye-catcher whether done in scrap fabrics or two different fabrics. Choose fabrics that contrast well with one another to achieve the push-pull effect of equally balanced light and dark areas.

Flock of Geese

Chain piece triangles together by feeding them through the machine without cutting the thread between the sets of pieces.

The joining edges of the triangles are cut on the bias. Take care in sewing and pressing to avoid distortion.

LIGHTNING, KINGS X, GOD'S EYE

These three designs can be made with the same two templates. Each unit square is pieced identically. A more pleasing effect may be achieved by placing the long side of the trapezoid template (#6) on the straight of grain. Care should be taken not to stretch the resulting bias outside edge.

Viewing Wall

Lightning

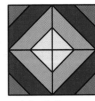

Kings X   God's Eye

PINWHEEL

- One template is used to construct this design.
- Use two or more fabrics.
- Place long edge of template on straight grain to avoid bias outer edges.

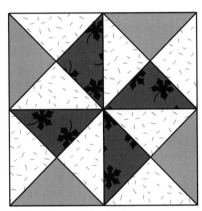

Pinwheel

CHECK POINT: SIZE COMPARISON

A pieced unit should be equal to the template.

Should equal / Unit Block

THE ANVIL

- A scrap block adds interest and integrates fabrics.
- Keep anvil color values similar to hold design together.
- After laying out design, sew pieces together a set at a time rather than chain piecing to avoid confusion in placement.

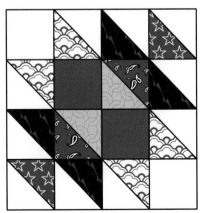

The Anvil

WHEELS

- Block gives feeling of movement.
- Long side of trapezoid (#6) may be cut with the straight of grain to add visual strength to the block. This will also stabilize bias edges of triangles.
- Trapezoid in this block is not reversible. Cut four identical shapes.

Wheels

STAR FLOWER

- Stars add crispness to a quilt when well done.
- All star points can be made by joining two small triangles or alternate star points can be cut using parallelogram template. Cut four identical points. Parallelogram pattern is not reversible in this block.
- Lay out design. Piece in rectangles rather than in rows.

Star Flower

WINDBLOWN SQUARE

• Block shows rhythm and depth.

• Combine two very similar background fabrics for added interest.

• Piece block in rectangles.

• Parallelogram is not reversible. Cut four identical parallelogram design pieces.

Windblown Square

YANKEE PUZZLE

• Block gives feeling of movement.

• Experiment with value placement to achieve varying effects.

• Piece in rectangles.

• Parallelogram is not reversible.

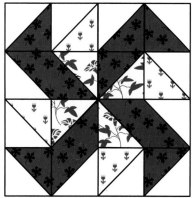

Yankee Puzzle

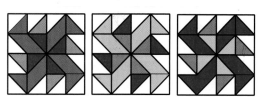

Yankee Puzzle variations

When more than four seams are being joined at an intersection, it is a good idea to pin the intersection first, and then machine baste the intersection (about 1") to make sure the seams align.

ANOTHER WAY OF DRAFTING

Sometimes a block has shapes that do not conform to the general Four-Patch format. It is easier then to draft the entire block full scale. In the case of Virginia Star by Hazel Carter the entire block is drawn on freezer paper.

Directions:

Use a 12" floor tile as a pattern to draw a 12" square on freezer paper.

Follow diagram to draw Virginia Star design.

Mark grain line on freezer paper.

Cut apart to make freezer paper templates.

Iron freezer paper to fabric.

Cut with rotary cutter, adding ¼" seam allowance.

This block gives you a wonderful opportunity to play with color and the effect of transparency, the look of one color blending visually with another. If a dark and a light triangle blend, the resulting area will be medium value. If a red and blue triangle cross, the resulting area will be purple. The scale of prints used should also be considered.

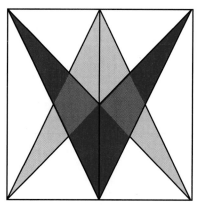

Virginia Star

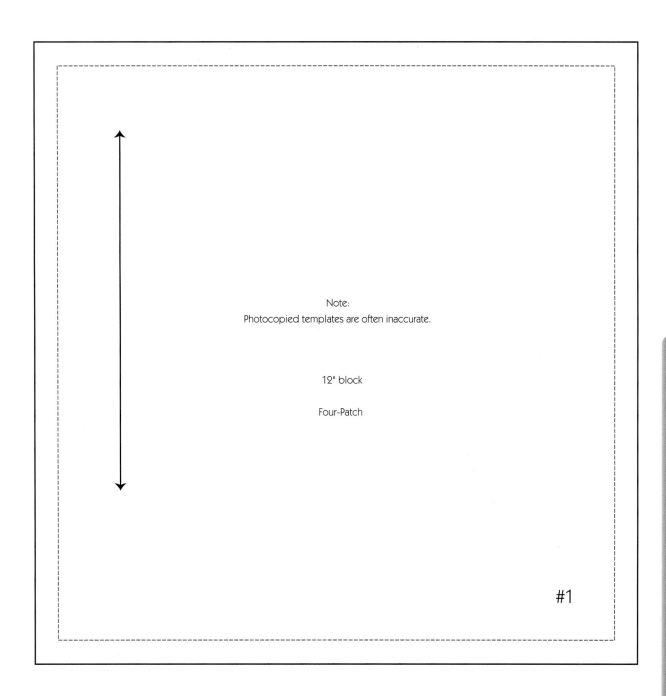

Note:
Photocopied templates are often inaccurate.

12" block

Four-Patch

#1

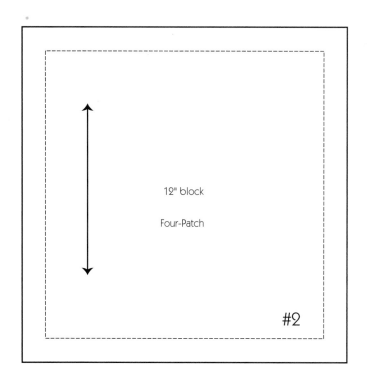

12" block

Four-Patch

#2

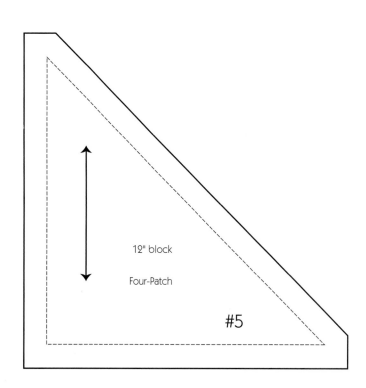

12" block

Four-Patch

#5

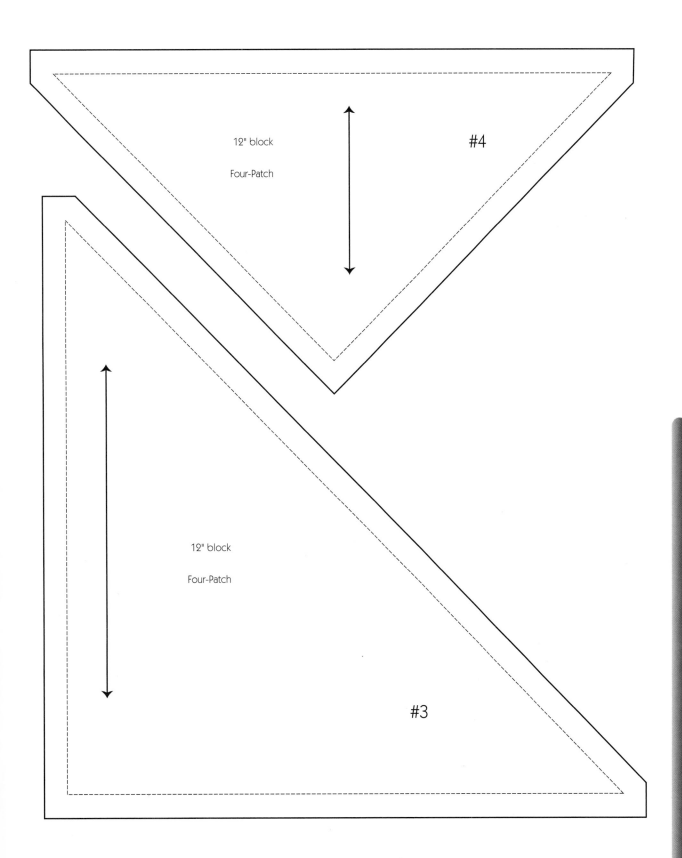

12" block

Four-Patch

#4

12" block

Four-Patch

#3

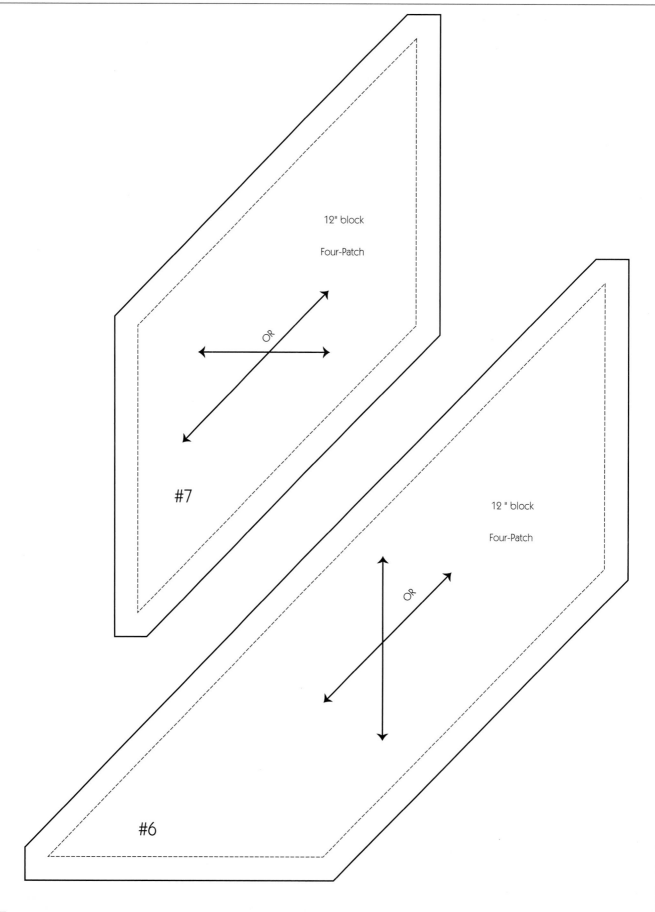

12" block

Four-Patch

OR

#7

12 " block

Four-Patch

OR

#6

*S*how-and-Tell opens the class and becomes a teaching/learning tool. It is exciting to see the color combinations of others, to see how a fabric can change in visual texture when pieced into a block, and to acknowledge that a good pressing job does make a big difference. Even if you are making a quilt in isolation, try to keep in touch with another quilter. Computer clubs are readily available for those of you who are on the Internet.

LESSON 2
PIECED BLOCKS

NINE-PATCH BLOCKS
•
SPEED PIECING
•
SETTING IN
•
DECORATIVE STRIPES
•
BACKING

NINE-PATCH BLOCKS

GOALS OF LESSON TWO

•Learn to recognize Nine-Patch blocks
•Make five different Nine-Patch blocks
•Back all blocks

SKILLS

•Recognizing Nine-Patch designs
•Speed piecing
•Working with stripes — Fussy Cutting
•Backing squares
•The quilt sandwich

The Nine-Patch block is divided into three rows of three squares. The unit block will be a 4" square plus seam allowance.

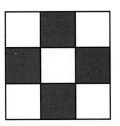

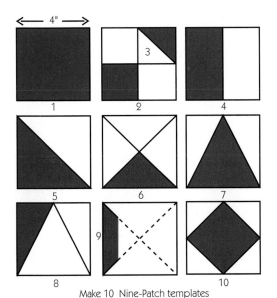

4"

Make 10 Nine-Patch templates

Find someone who will share the joy that comes with each new finished block! Everyone needs a quilting buddy.

ALBUM

Center could be used as a signature area or for creative piecing or quilting. Repeat blocks would make an interesting quilt with secondary designs emerging.

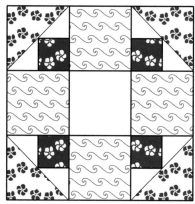

Album

CHECK POINT: SIZE COMPARISON

Slight inaccuracies multiply if not caught and corrected. After two small triangles (#3) have been sewn to small square (#2), compare size with triangle (#5). They should be equal.

THE OHIO STAR

A block that is a recognized favorite. The block dates back to the late 1800s. A dark background with a light design is often unexpected and successful. Star can be cut from one fabric or many. Value of star points must be similar to hold design together.

The Ohio Star

> ### HINT
> #### SPEED PIECING
> Be alert to repeating shapes and save time! If a block has many repeating shapes, time can be saved by speed piecing.

RAIL FENCE

Select four fabrics, light to dark values. Cut one strip 1½" across the fabric width from each. Carefully sew strips together. Cut into squares using unit block template. Sew block, alternating direction of squares.

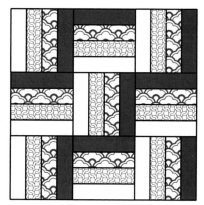

Rail Fence

54/40 OR FIGHT

In 54/40 or Fight there are 10 identical sets of squares which can accurately be speed pieced. Instead of cutting individual squares and seaming them two by two, a pair of fabric strips can be joined and then cut into rectangles.

54/40 or Fight

Select two contrasting fabrics. Measure width of appropriate template #2. Determine length of strip by measuring side of template by the number of squares. Cut strips. Sew strips. Press. Cut into rectangles. Reposition alternate rectangles, matching seam line. Sew into squares.

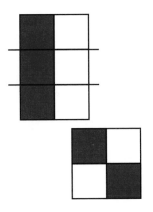

BIRD OF PARADISE

Bird of Paradise is identical in design to 54/40 or Fight, but it has more fabric variety. To speed piece, one fabric strip is cut from the lighter, constant fabric. Individually cut fabric squares are placed, right sides together, on the strip and sewn.

Bird of Paradise

ON TEMPLATE

Mark seam line angles with a ⅛" paper punched hole. Trim extending seam allowance to ¼".

PIECING STAR POINTS

Mark angles on fabric using a small hole in the template and disappearing fabric marking pen. Match marked angles. Sew one star point to background. Press seam open carefully. Add other star point to opposite side. Compare size of pieced square to unit block.

Unit Block
Nine-Patch
12" block

HINT

Add reference marks to templates. When sharp angles are joined, it is often difficult to align the two pieces accurately. Reference marks placed on the joining fabric pieces will help to create a perfectly matched seam.

MAPLE LEAF

Appliqué stem to block before piecing. Cut a 1" x 6" strip. Fold raw edges to center. Press. Stitch on edges or use invisible blind hem appliqué (Les. 4).

Maple Leaf

HINT

Four 6" leaves can be pieced using templates 2 and 3.

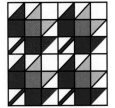

Experiment with block rotation

SPOOLS

Great design to be used in a quilt. Stripe works well as the thread. Uses "setting in" piecing technique.

Spools

SETTING IN

Stitching will only be on actual seam line. Mark end of seam line with reference dots using disappearing pen. Match dots on spool to dots on thread. Stitch from dot to dot, securing stitching at ends. Repeat three more times. Pivot fabric. Match remaining edges. Stitch to end of piece. Press. Do not press seams open.

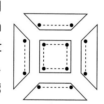

FUSSY CUTTING

Eleanor Burns from *Quilt in a Day*, coined the term "fussy cutting," which describes the manner that stripes or large prints are individually and identically cut for dramatic effects. The process requires more time and care, but the results are rewarding.

CARD TRICK

This intriguing block requires only two triangle templates and simple piecing. Using the fussy cutting technique, you will have sensational results! For a dramatic cut, choose either a striped fabric or one with an interesting large print.

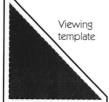

Viewing template

Make a viewing template by cutting away the center of the

large triangle template, # 5. Take care to leave the seam allowance, the outer edge, in place.

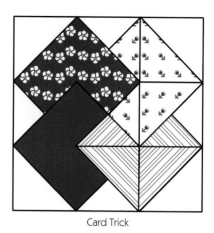

Card Trick

Place template on desired fabric design element. Cut one triangle, disregarding grain line.

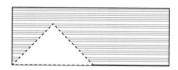

Use cut fabric triangle to cut 3 more identical pieces. To make sure that design will fall properly, temporarily arrange pieces to form a square placed on point. Cut two large triangles into smaller triangles by placing the small template on large cut triangle. Discard small waste triangles.

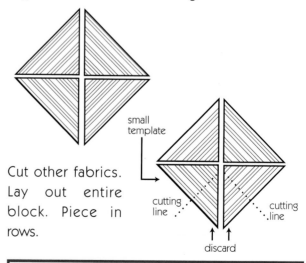

small template

Cut other fabrics. Lay out entire block. Piece in rows.

cutting line

cutting line

discard

HINT
Fabrics with a definite pattern should be cut by the fussy cutting method for best visual presentation.

THE QUILT SANDWICH

To be a quilt, by definition of the word, a design must be sandwiched with a layer of batting placed over a backing fabric and held together with stitches. Your pieced blocks are about ready to qualify.

The backing fabric that you purchased must cover the back of all the blocks plus the back of the sashing that you will choose later. If your plan includes borders, backing fabric must also be available to cover the back of the borders.

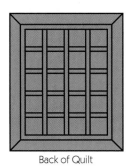

Back of Quilt

DIVIDING THE BACKING FABRIC

Bed size	Back of blocks	Set aside yardage
Twin	3¼ yards	4¼ yards
Double/Queen	3¼ yards	7¾ yards
King	3½ yards	8½ yards

The backing fabric will be divided: fabric for back of quilt blocks, fabric for back of sashing, fabric for back of borders (optional).

The fabric for the back of the blocks will be used immediately. The remaining backing fabric will be set aside, labeled, and put away for future use.

THE BATTING

Batting is the filling in a quilt which gives it dimension as well as warmth. You may possibly have purchased it from a store that sold it from a large roll, but generally batting comes packaged in a snug roll. It should be opened a few hours before cutting to allow it to relax. This has been known to be a problem in a home shared with cats, so take adequate precautions.

The batting squares will be cut just a bit larger than the finished size of the block, 12". An individual floor tile which measures 12" makes a good template for cutting batting as well as for block drafting. You don't need to be too exact when cutting batting, as you want the squares of batting to be a tad larger than 12" anyway.

Four of the quilt blocks require a little extra working room: Log Cabin, Diagonal String, Clamshell, and Crazy Patch. Batting and backing squares (15") will be prepared for these blocks. These larger blocks will be trimmed later.

> **HINT**
> Batting is cut close to the size of the finished block to eliminate bulk in the seam allowance.

CUTTING BATTING

Four layers of batting can be cut at one time with the rotary cutter. You may have to initially refold the batting if necessary to align the edges.

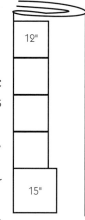

- Lay batting on cutting board.
- Use 12" floor tile as template.
- Cut with rotary cutter.
- Cut along the length to save remaining length for the long strips needed later.
- Cut sixteen 12" squares for twin, double, or queen.
- Cut twenty-one 12" squares for king.
- Cut four 15" squares for any size quilt.

THE BACK OF THE BLOCKS

The fabric for the back of the blocks, will be made into squares also. Since the quilting process may draw the back up slightly, the squares will be cut 13" by 13" which is slightly larger than the pieced block to allow a little "squirm" room.

•Cut 13" squares: cut 16 for twin, double, or queen; cut 21 for king.

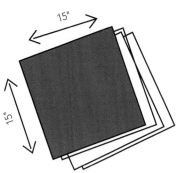

•Cut 15" squares: cut 4 for any size quilt.

PREPARING BACKING

The back fabric will be torn into two long 13" strips. This is the easiest way to get a good, straight strip. Most 100% cotton fabrics tear well on the lengthwise grain. After the strips have been torn, they will be cut in the other direction with the rotary cutter to form squares.

To tear backings: Tear off the selvage and discard. Measure 13" across fabric. Snip into fabric to start tearing. Measure 13" more, snip again. Measure 15" and snip once more. Gently tear the 13" strips .

Use the rotary cutter and gridded mat board to cut the strips into 13" squares.

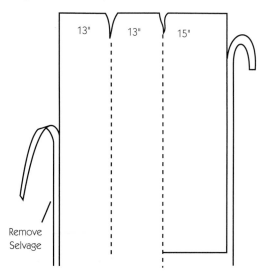

Remove Selvage

Tear one 15" strip 60" long, cut into four 15" squares.

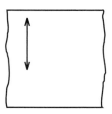

By having torn two sides and cut two sides, you will be able to determine lengthwise grain when assembling the blocks. The torn edges are the lengthwise grain.

QUILT SANDWICHES

The finished block designs will now be made into quilt sandwiches in preparation for quilting.

To make a quilt sandwich:
•Press backing square. Center batting on wrong side of backing. Place pressed quilt block on batting. Press gently with a warm iron. Secure with straight pins.

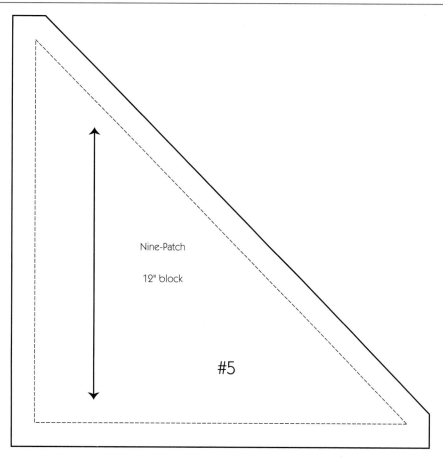

Nine-Patch

12" block

#5

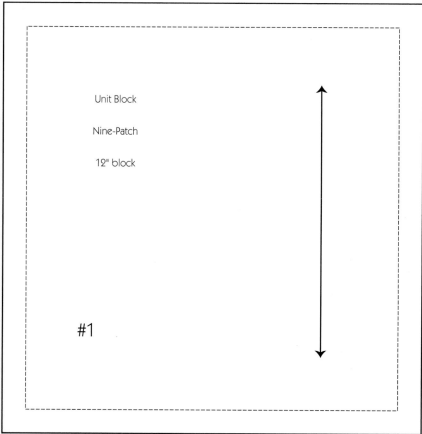

Unit Block

Nine-Patch

12" block

#1

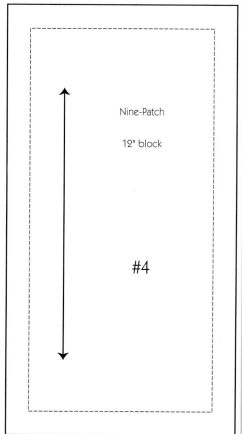

Nine-Patch

12" block

#4

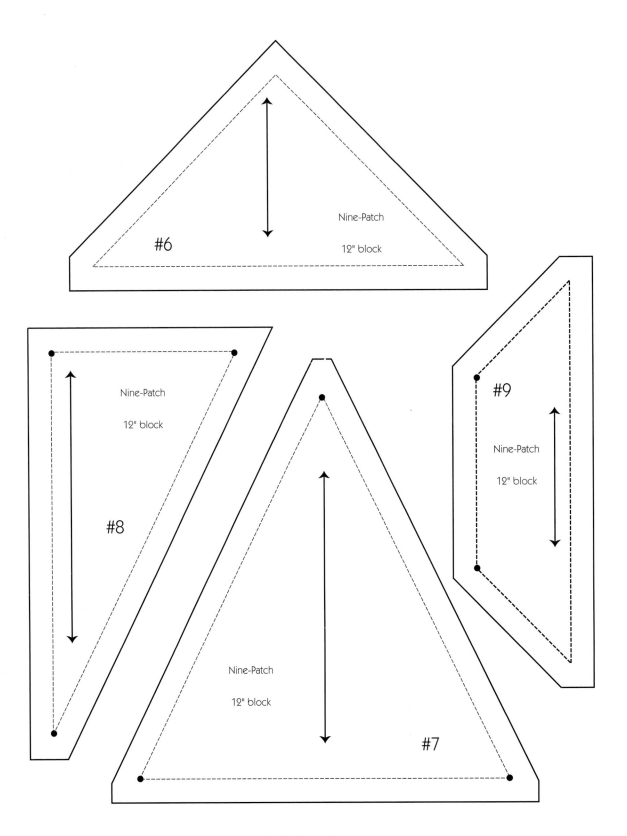

#6 Nine-Patch 12" block

#8 Nine-Patch 12" block

#7 Nine-Patch 12" block

#9 Nine-Patch 12" block

● Indicates Small Hole Punch

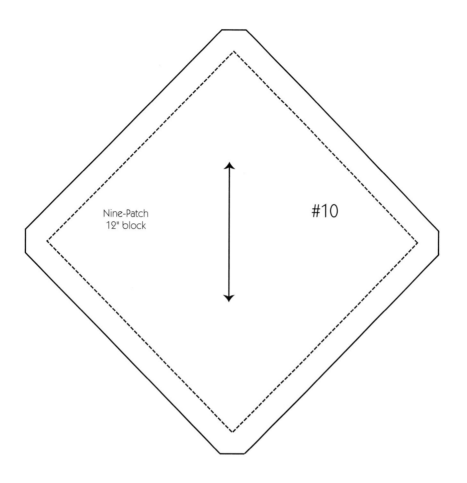

Nine-Patch
12" block

#10

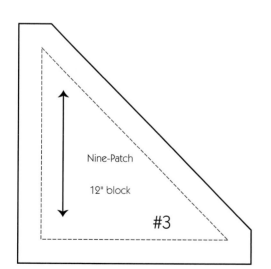

Nine-Patch

12" block

#3

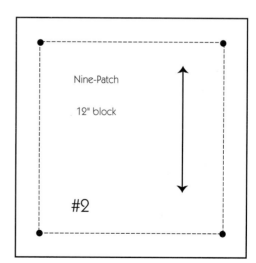

Nine-Patch

12" block

#2

● Small hole punch for spools block.

T he beauty of a block increases with each step of the quiltmaking process. Quilting adds the finishing touch to a design. It can make patterns leap from the surface as well as push a fabric quietly into the background. Quilting gives depth, texture, and interest to a block. Quilting is also necessary to hold the layers of fabric and batting together.

MACHINE QUILTING

GOAL OF LESSON THREE
•Quilt all 10 pieced blocks
EXERCISES:
•Quilting wit h the regular presser foot
•Quilting with the even-feed foot
•Quilting with a darning foot

SKILLS
•Stitching in the seam line
•Free-motion quilting
•Straight line quilting
•Echo quilting
•Continuous line designs
•Embellishments

Machine quilting does not have to mimic hand quilting. It can be exciting in its own right. On the other hand, if you love to hand quilt, you can combine hand and machine quilting in the same block.

If you like the look of hand quilting but don't want to do it, many of the newer sewing machines have a stitch that looks like hand quilting. It may not appear as a decorative stitch but rather as a tension adjustment. The top tension is tightened to pull up the bobbin thread. Invisible thread is used in the top and a light gray in the bobbin. Ask your dealer to show you.

STANDARDS OF GOOD WORKMANSHIP

•Blocks should be smooth and free from puckers.
•Quilting stitch length should be uniform and similar to other visible stitches.
•Straight quilting lines should be straight.
•Curved quilting lines should be smooth.
•The amount of quilting in blocks should be consistent.
•Beginning and ending of quilting stitches should be unobtrusive.
•Quilting stitches should lock in batting:
   Bobbin thread should not pull up to top surface.
   Top thread should not pull to back.
•All marking lines should be removed.

Quilting can make you feel good about a block. You will be making creative decisions that will make your blocks unique. I like to think of each block as a short story. Imagine different ways to complete the block. Help each block be all it can be. Think of the different ways a block could be quilted. Which type of quilting would make the block spectacular? Once you become familiar with machine quilting techniques, you will find them fun and relaxing. The hard part will be stopping!

Before starting to quilt your blocks, check out a few tools and marking techniques.

MARKING ON A QUILT

Marking a design on a quilt involves two things: getting the design markings *on* the quilt; getting the design markings *off* the quilt.

MARKING TOOLS

Free-motion quilting and stitching in the seam line do not require marking designs on the fabric. However, some straight line and other patterns do require that a line be drawn or a design transferred to fabric. There are several tools available for this:

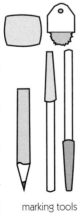

marking tools

•A disappearing marking pen, generally purple. This line disappears within 12 hours, so it is recommended for short-term projects. I have used the purple disappearing pen for over 20 years and have had only one bad experience. I failed to test a pen on a scrap of the batik that I was marking. When the ink disappeared, so did most of the color from the fabric. I quickly gathered up all my purple marking pens. There were four of them. I tested each on the batik and found that only one caused a problem. I guess it was a faulty pen. I still use disappearing ink pens, but I test first on a scrap. I also spritz the area and wipe it with a towel when I have finished quilting.

•A water soluble pen, generally blue or pink. The line lasts until it is removed with water. Unless the ink is thoroughly removed with clear water, the ink can be forced into the batting, causing it to reappear later.

•Pencil. Not recommended for marking machine stitched designs. It is hard to remove, and distracting, especially if the quilting line is a off its mark.

•Chalk. Available in several colors. It can generally be rubbed off easily, but test before using.

ADDITIONAL MARKING METHODS

There are methods of design transfer that do not involve marking on fabric. I highly recommend these.

DELI OR FOOD WRAP

This delightfully thin, transparent paper comes in a dispenser box and can be found in large discount food stores. Besides making a wonderful pressing cloth and machine quilting stabilizer, it is great for transferring quilting designs. It tears away after being stitched without leaving a trace of paper behind. It can also pass through the copy machine if trimmed to 8½" by 11" and temporarily glued with rubber cement across the top and bottom to a piece of copy paper.

FREEZER PAPER

Freezer paper is also great for transferring designs. Because it is translucent, designs can be traced onto the dull surface, ironed in place, and then stitched. After stitching, a light spritz of water will soften the paper for easy removal. Another freezer paper method is to cut simple shapes and stitch around them. The pattern shapes are reusable.

Designs can be copied onto the freezer paper in the copy machine if the freezer paper is first ironed to fabric and cut to 8½" by 11". Peel freezer paper off fabric and reuse fabric with fresh freezer paper for the next design. Keep all threads trimmed from fabric.

PRACTICE QUILTING

These exercises will give you confidence to start quilting your blocks.

MAKE SEVERAL PRACTICE SQUARES

Make three 12" practice quilting sandwiches out of muslin or any solid colored fabric. Pin the layers of fabric and batting together with straight pins in the corners and center portion. Play with each technique until you are comfortable and ready to  move on. If it takes more time and space to feel confident, make more quilt sandwiches and keep on quilting!

STRAIGHT STITCHING

The initial stitching on the quilt block sandwich is generally straight stitching to anchor and secure the three layers. The stitching will be in the seam line. The square integrity of the block should be maintained without puckers either on the front of the block or on the back side. You will decide whether your machine requires the use of the even feed foot for this stitching or if the regular presser foot will give equally satisfactory results in keeping the block smooth.

EXERCISE ONE: STRAIGHT STITCHING — REGULAR PRESSER FOOT

Back shows evidence of puckers.

Machine set up:
- Regular presser foot
- Needle: Jeans 70/10

Thread:
- Invisible nylon in needle
- Thread in bobbin to match back of practice square

Feed dogs up

Stitch length #2. Stitch length should be visually similar to those created with free-motion stitching.

PRACTICE

Stitch two lines forming a cross through the centers of a practice square. Check top for signs of bobbin thread pulling up to top surface. If so, loosen top tension slightly. Thread bobbin finger if you have one, putting more tension on the bobbin thread. Check back of block for gathering or puckers. If so, loosen top tension slightly. If loops of nylon thread appear on the back, thread the top of the machine again, making sure the presser foot is in the up position. Try stitching again. If loops do not disappear, try tightening the top tension.

EXERCISE TWO: USING THE EVEN FEED FOOT

Repeat exercise one using the even feed foot. Compare results and decide which foot will do the best job for you. Make note of tension settings for future reference.

FREE-MOTION STITCHING

Free-motion stitching is a new experience for many. The feed dogs which have always moved the fabric along, are now dropped or disengaged, leaving the movement of the fabric up to the operator of the sewing machine. The presser foot which typically holds the fabric in place is now replaced by the bouncing darning foot. The pressure on the foot pedal still determines the motor speed and the rate at which the stitches are produced. The stitch length is determined by the speed of the motor and the rate at which you move the fabric rather than the stitch length regulator. Free-motion stitching is like drawing on fabric with a needle. It is the fabric that moves while the needle position remains stationary.

The thought of all this freedom may seem intimidating at first. There are many advantages to free-motion stitching, however. Curves both large and small can be manipulated without turning the fabric around in circles. This is a big advantage especially when quilting large pieces. This is your free spirit dancing across the blocks. If you like to be creative, you will love this.

Free-motion quilting adds your signature to the quilt. Like penmanship, no two people do free-motion stitching exactly alike.

The success of this type of stitching lies in running the sewing machine moderately fast while gliding the fabric slowly and evenly.

Free Motion Quilting

Moving the fabric too rapidly produces skipped stitches. Moving the fabric too slowly produces tiny stitches or even a pile up of stitches.

> *Another ditty to sing: Fairly fast goes the motor. Slow and graceful moves the block!*

When stitching, keep the lower edge of the block parallel with the front of the machine. Move the block forward, backward, side to side, or in a circular path. Do not turn the block round and round like a steering wheel. Take the time to set aside an hour or so to get in tune with the rhythms and techniques of free-motion machine quilting. If you 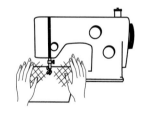 have a quilting buddy, invite her to come over with her sewing machine for a quilting party. If you have the opportunity to take a one day class in machine quilting, do that.

EXERCISE THREE: FREE-MOTION QUILTING
Machine set up:
•Flat quilting surface: cabinet, tray, or removable flat bed.
•Needle: Quilting Needle size 7.5.
•Thread: Regular sewing thread or decorative rayon threads.
•Feed Dogs: Dropped (See your sewing machine manual.) Some machines have a small plate that covers the feed dogs. This often crowds the space between the foot and the throat plate. If this occurs, set stitch length at 0 and forget about covering the feed dogs.

Darning foot: This is a spring-loaded foot that holds the fabric to the bed of the machine for good stitch formation at the end of the downward stroke. After the stitch is formed it bounces up again so the fabric can be moved freely.

> ### HINT
> Two 3" squares of rug grip placed under your fingers on the quilt surface will help to move the fabric along without making your hands hot. Wearing golf gloves to move fabric works well, too, for larger projects. If a darning foot did not come with your machine, search for one. Have your model number or even your machine, if it is portable, with you. Darning feet are available for high shank, low shank, and slant needle machines.

Try each of the following patterns. Notice how quickly your skills improve! Add some patterns of your own.

MEANDER STITCH
You will be using this motion frequently. Say to yourself, 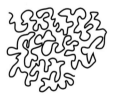 "curves that don't cross," or "jigsaw puzzle pieces," or "squiggles." Repeat your phrase until the motion comes freely. Initially you may get a few angles. These will disappear with practice. You will be using your upper arm muscles for this pattern.

MINI-MEANDER
You will be doing this with your fingertips. Curves that don't cross are the same pattern as above but miniaturized.  Notice how different it feels. While this generally looks great, it is very slow going and tends to make your quilt a little stiff. Reserve this for small areas.

NERVOUS NELLY

Use the same curves that don't cross but this time set the machine at #2 width zigzag. This stitch rapidly builds up thread on the quilt surface. Works well with metallic thread if you want a densely quilted area with sparkle.

Nervous Nelly

LOOP DE LOOPS

Think in terms of making cursive e's and L's with this pattern. Try to keep the design free flowing rather than compact.

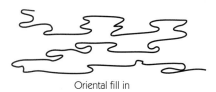

Loop de Loops

ORIENTAL FILL IN

Think curves that don't cross and space. It looks Oriental or like water. If you turn it on its side, it looks like a cactus. Try it!

Oriental fill in

CIRCLES

When filling in an area with circles you might think of figure 8's This is continuous stitching so you will have to retrace some of your lines to make the next circle.

OTHER FREE-MOTION MIND SETS...

Practice a bit more. This time try free-motion stitching on a drawn line. Slow your pace, increase your concentration, and don't forget to breathe.

QUILTING A PATTERN

There will be times when a blank area will benefit by filling it in with a specific design. In Grandmother's Fan, Lesson Four, the area surrounding the fan is too large to be left unquilted, and the block will be enhanced with the addition of the ribbon pattern.

"How am I going to do this?"
By Hand? If you love hand quilting, you could quilt this pattern by hand. Stitches that are small and even are lovely even in a machine stitched sampler.

By Machine? If you choose to do the same design by machine, great! Practice a little on a scrap until you are comfortable following the design with free-motion stitching.

The Light Box. The light box enables you to see and trace a design onto fabric. The design is taped to the top of the box and traced directly onto the fabric.

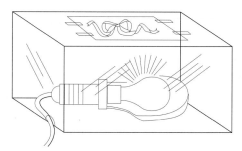

CONTINUOUS-LINE STITCHING

Machine quilting flows smoothly when there are no stops and starts to break the rhythm. Even elaborate patterns can be designed and stitched following a continuous line which twists and turns.

Hari Walner has designed a continuous-line pattern, "All Directions," for your enjoyment. Practice it now. Use it to quilt the large corners of the Double Four-Patch design.

Transfer design. Follow the traced design with your finger until you feel the flow of the pattern. Unthread your machine. Stitch pattern line without thread until you are comfortable with the flow. Thread machine with matching thread and use a slow and even stitching speed. Use rug gripper to help move fabric. Keep your wrists relaxed. Many continuous-line designs are available as stencils.

All Directions 5½"
All Directions designed by Hari Walner.

IT'S TIME TO QUILT YOUR BLOCKS

Start with any one of the sandwiched blocks. Thread the needle with invisible nylon thread for seam line quilting. (Change to regular or decorative thread for other machine quilting.) Fill bobbin with thread to match backing. Attach even feed foot or use regular presser foot. Stitch in the seam line to anchor all three layers of block. Anchor stitch several blocks as long as machine is set up.

SEAM LINE QUILTING

Seam line stitching is done first to anchor and stabilize the three layers of the quilt block. Exercises one and two helped you to determine setup and which foot will work best for you on your machine. Do horizontal lines first, vertical lines next, and then diagonal lines, if any. Stitching may go from one edge of the block to the other. Seam allowances do not need to be left unquilted.

STARTING AND STOPPING QUILTING LINES

In some blocks quilting will originate in the center of the block. Start with a very few tiny stitches or use the lock stitch on your machine. Threads will be secured and ends can then be cut off. Trim thread ends as you go to keep your work clean.

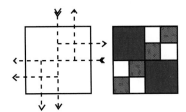

WHAT NOW?

Seam line quilting can be the only quilting on a block or it can be just the beginning. Now the quilt sandwich is stable. The batting will not shift when the quilt is washed. But do not stop now. Add the frosting! Contemplate additional quilting.

Hand quilters have traditionally chosen to quilt ¼" on either side of the seam line. In machine quilting this would require many starts and stops. In its place a different quilting format has emerged.

After the block has been anchored, the design area is often left unquilted or minimally quilted and the background is quilted with either free-motion stitching or straight line quilting in thread to match the fabric.

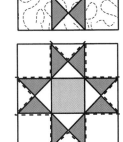

Free-motion stitching suppresses the background or negative space and gives prominence to the positive space, the design itself. Try quilting with various forms of free-motion stitching. Straight lines can be used to simply outline a design. Use the side of the presser foot as a guide for stitching.

Straight line quilting can alter the appearance of a block! Lines can cut through the background areas of a block. A straight line design can be stitched over the entire block surface, ignoring the original piecing lines. Lines can divide space systematically by halves and quarters. Echo Quilting uses the presser foot as a guide and continues with rows of stitching evenly spaced.

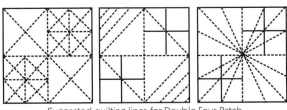

Suggested quilting lines for Double Four-Patch

THE PIVOT LINE

To get a crisp angle when quilting lines change direction, draw a pivot line at the desired angle with a fabric marking pen before starting. Quilt to pivot line, pivot, and finish quilting.

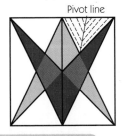
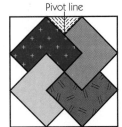

Lois Smith's Machine Quiltmaking

QUILTING DESIGNS AND IDEAS

Quilting designs and ideas are endless and personal. Try to keep the amount of quilting in each block similar so that shrinkage due to quilting will be uniform. You will develop your own style of machine quilting. There are no hard and fast rules, but a few guidelines may help you in making design choices.

- Keep starts and stops to a minimum.
- Use quilting designs that fit your quilt theme.
- Soft curving lines complement straight line piecing.
- Straight line quilting complements curved piecing.
- Design motifs can be cut from freezer paper and ironed in place as a stitching guide. These are reusable. If you are undecided, lay a clear 12" template plastic square over your pieced block. With an erasable magic marker you can draw and try out several different quilting ideas. Choose the one you like the best and get started.

FREE-MOTION RELAXED ECHOES

The Kachina Dancer is echo quilted using free-motion stitching and the darning foot. The first line is quilted about ¼" from the design. As the quilting progresses, the echo lines become more and more relaxed, losing the contours of the original design.

Echo Quilting

DECORATIVE MACHINE STITCHES

Experiment with some of the stitches on your machine. They are fun to try and use. By changing the length and width of the stitches you may get entirely different looks.

Decorative Machine Stitches

COUCHED THREADS OR BEADING

Heavy threads or beads on a string can be stitched in place with invisible nylon thread and a zigzag stitch. This adds strength to a design line. Take care to fasten the ends of these materials by weaving them into batting with a tapestry needle.

Couched Threads/Beading

EMBELLISHMENTS

Beads and other novelties can add interest to the quilt surface. Attach them securely.

Embellishments

Half of your quilt blocks are already finished if you have followed the suggested pace. Have you noticed how much easier it is at this point to select appropriate fabrics for each block? Your confidence is building!

The next four blocks require very little quilting. You will be surprised at the speed in which these great blocks can be completed!

The blocks in this chapter are not pieced like the Four-Patch and Nine-Patch block designs. The technique is called quilt as you go. Instead of sewing just two fabrics together, you will be stitching your cut pieces and the batting and backing all at one time. When you have finished your block, it will be completed and quilted. What a bargain!

QUILT AS YOU GO

GOALS OF LESSON FOUR

Complete four single design blocks
- Strip quilting
- Log Cabin
- Dresden Plate
- Granny's Fan

SKILLS

- Quilt As You Go
- Assembly line sewing
- Appliqué
- Marking quilting designs

STRIP QUILTING

Strip quilting is probably the easiest and most versatile technique in the whole quilt. This type of quilting is popular in quilted clothing as well as in decorator items.

In this block, 1½" strips of fabric will be sewn through the batting and backing simultaneously, creating a block of many fabrics. A 15" backing and a 15" batting will be used as the foundation. Since the block itself may tend to skew a bit during construction, the added inches are for your protection. The block will later be trimmed to match the other quilt blocks in size. (Save the trimmed scraps for use in the crazy patch later.)

Fabrics:

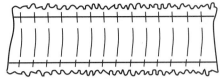

- Use a wide variety of prints and solids.
- Use light, medium, and dark values.
- Use your zinger sparingly.
- Just for fun, place strips in a bag and use them in the order that you draw them from the bag.

Cut:

- Ten to twelve 1½" strips, the width of the fabric
- Use your rotary cutter and practice accuracy.

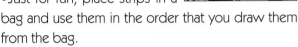

Prepare foundation by layering 15" backing and 15" batting.

Sew:

- Place the first strip diagonally across the batting sandwich, ends touching opposite corners, strip right side up.
- Lay second strip on top of first, right sides together.

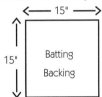

- Sew right edge with ¼" seam allowance.
- Sew through strips, batting, and backing.
- Use walking foot for a smoother back.
- Flip top strip to right-side-up position. Finger crease seam line. Pin raw edge in place to hold strip flat momentarily.

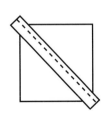

- Cut off extra extending strip fabric.
- Place next strip on top of previous strip, right-sides together, reposition pins, sew, flip, reposition pins.

Continue in this manner until one-half of block is filled. Repeat for other half.

CREATIVE ADDITIONS

- Gather the edges of a strip before sewing it to the foundation.

- Skinny Strip

Place new strip on top of previous strip. Offset raw edges, previous raw edge extending beyond new strip. Sew. Trim extending excess, if desired. Flip new strip into position. Previous strip will be skinny.

- Angled Strips also called irregular strings. After initial two strips are sewn, angle new strip and sew. Trim excess. Flip new strip. Add next strip, angling in opposite direction. Sew, trim, flip, etc.

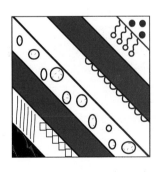

- Insertions

Add 3-D embellishments in the seam line between strips: prairie points, rickrack, etc. Add loops of decorative thread or yarn.

LOG CABIN BLOCKS

The Log Cabin blocks are a study in value contrast — light vs. dark. They require carefully graded values plus precision cutting and sewing techniques to achieve a block that is crisp and square. This version, Sunshine and Shadows, features a strong diagonal line separating the light from dark fabrics.

Value can be sorted by squinting at the fabrics in a dim light. The early morning is a good time for this as the eyes are only partially opened anyway.

Fabric swatches can be photocopied, reducing them to black-and-white or gray scale. Values then become apparent.

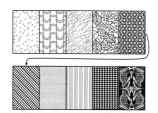

Some fabrics contain sharply contrasting values in the same fabric. They are hard to sort accurately. This type of fabric will always remain spotty and not read properly. Eliminate them in the Log Cabin.

Traditionally, the square in the center was assumed to be the fire or chimney in the Log Cabin, and therefore, seen as red or yellow. The center can be any fabric, but it should be zippy.

The Log Cabin design is presented in two sizes: a 12" block to be constructed quilt as you go or an assembly line technique making four 6" blocks which will be sewn together to complete a 12" block. Each requires fabric strips cut the width of the fabric.

QUILT-AS-YOU-GO METHOD LOG CABIN

FABRICS

Select 5 graduated light value fabrics.
Select 5 graduated dark value fabrics.

Sort each group by value.
- Cut 2" strip of darkest light.
- Cut 2" strip of darkest dark.
- Cut 1½" strips of remaining fabrics.
- Cut one 2½" square of fire or chimney.

CONSTRUCTION OVERVIEW

Start with a 15" backing/batting sandwich. Center chimney square on sandwich by drawing diagonal lines across batting and placing square with corners touching lines. Logs will be added around the center square in a clockwise direction. Add two matching light logs starting with the lightest value. Add two matching dark logs starting with the lightest dark value. Repeat using all four values of light and dark. Finish with 2" strips.

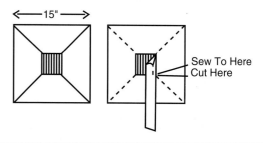

Sew To Here
Cut Here

> **HINT**
> Accuracy pays dividends. Keep a small ruler by your machine and measure as you go.

SEWING

Sew with a very accurate ¼" seam allowance. Place lightest strip on right side of chimney square, right sides together. Start sewing ¼" from top of strip. Stop sewing ¼" from bottom of square. (This eliminates stitching spurs on back.) Secure threads by starting and stopping with very tight stitches. Trim strip to equal length of square. Turn strip into position, finger crease seam line. Pin to hold strip in place. Sew second strip the width of center

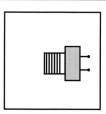

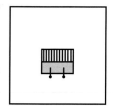

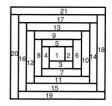

square plus first log. Continue adding two darks and two lights.

If you have a limited number of fabrics, choose five values from light to dark. Arrange fabrics from light to dark on one side. Arrange fabrics from dark to light on opposite.

Or use one fabric for one side of Log Cabin. Grade fabrics from light to dark for opposite side.

ASSEMBLY LINE MINI LOG CABIN

Assembly line piecing is efficient and accurate. This mini Log Cabin is pieced without batting or backing. Four 6" Log Cabin sections will be made simultaneously by the assembly line method and then joined to make the quilt block of your choice. It will then be sandwiched and quilted.

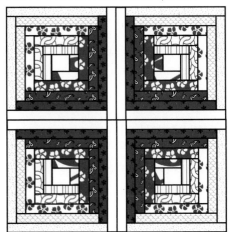

The Sunshine and Shadow effect becomes more apparent when four blocks are joined.

FABRICS
- •Cut 4 centers: 1½" square.
- •Cut 5 graduated light strips 1".
- •Cut 5 graduated dark strips 1".

CONSTRUCTION
Lay four centers on lightest strip. Sew right edge with very accurate ¼" seam allowance. Cut light

strip equal in depth of centers. Open pair and press seam away from center. Lay combined squares on same light strip and seam right edge. Rotate developing design and lay on first dark strip. Continue rotating and changing fabric strips until each side has logs.

ARRANGE BLOCKS
- •Place all darks in the center; or
- •place all lights in the center; or
- •position all four blocks identically.

PREPARE TO SEW
- •Measure squares to make sure they will make a 12" finished block.
  - •Add an extra strip through the center if needed.
  - •Layer block, batting, backing.
  - •Quilt in the seam line, over all diagonal grid, or anything you choose.

INVISIBLE APPLIQUÉ

Appliqué is the term used when a shape is placed on another piece of fabric and stitched in place. In the Dresden Plate, the pieced plate will be appliquéd to a foundation fabric.

In quilts it is generally preferable to have the raw edges turned under before the piece is applied or appliquéd. This gives a stronger edge and is more in keeping with traditional appliqué. There will be no concern over ravels and exposed edges.

There are several methods of machine appliqué that work well. Your machine will probably be the determining factor.

BLIND HEM APPLIQUÉ ⎯⎯^⎯⎯^⎯⎯^⎯⎯^

Blind hem appliqué can be almost invisible on the surface of the quilt. Invisible nylon thread and the blind hem stitch of the machine make this possible. The blind hem, machine foot is not used in this process, although your machine guide book may suggest it.

MACHINE SET UP

Needle fine and sharp. Jeans #70. Thread the needle with invisible nylon thread. The bobbin thread will match the quilt backing. The machine will be set for blind hem stitch.

Other adjustments: reduce stitch length to a very tight stitch (1½); reduce zigzag swing measurably (1½ or less); reduce top tension if bobbin thread pulls to top.

Select a reference mark on your basic foot that allows you to follow the appliqué edge easily. You may have to move your needle position. The straight stitches will fall invisibly in the foundation. The jump-over stitches will fall in the appliqué.

HINT

The jump-over stitch width, —^—, closes as the stitch length becomes smaller. The smaller the straight machine stitches are, the straighter the jump-over stitch is. A small, close jump-over stitch is desired.

CREATIVE OPTIONS

• Try a blanket stitch instead of the blind hem stitch.
• Use a straight stitch on the very edge of the appliqué.
• Use a decorative stitch to secure appliqué.
• Use a decorative thread, increase zigzag width.
• Use two threads going through the same needle eye.
• Experiment with different stitch lengths.

THE DRESDEN PLATE

The Dresden Plate block has always been a favorite with quiltmakers. The machine techniques create

Dresden Plate

self-faced petals with lovely sharp points or smooth curves depending upon your preference. An entire quilt can easily be made with just this one block. I once made a quilt for a friend using her lifetime of fabrics. The fabrics ranged from cotton to wool including denim and chiffons. I grouped the fabrics so that each plate had similar weight fabrics. It worked fine!

The Dresden Plate is a combination block. The petals are pieced into a plate and then appliquéd onto a foundation. The ends of the petals include a self facing for simple and foolproof finishing.

The template for any size Dresden Plate can be drafted using a compass and paper:
• draw a circle the size of desired plate. (5½" radius for 12" block.)
• Use same center point, draw circle: 1" radius.
• Divide large circle into 16ths.
• Fold paper into quarters.
• Divide one quarter into fourths.

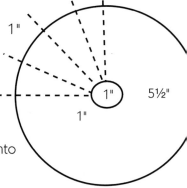

POINTED PETAL TEMPLATE

Start with one section:
• Remove the 1" from the lower edge.
• Redraw curved outer edge to straight edge.
• Add ¼" seam allowance to all sides.
• Make and label template.

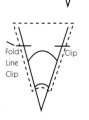

CURVED PETAL TEMPLATE

Start with one section:
• Extend long sides of petal ½".
• Connect extended lines with straight line.
• Mark fold line 1" from top edge with seam line clips.
• Add seam allowances.

CENTER TEMPLATES
• 3½" circle becomes center cutting template.
• 2½" circle becomes pressing template.
• Use tagboard or heat resistant template material.

FABRICS
• Foundation: 13" square (a little extra squirm room has been allowed).
• Petals: Cut 16 petals which will contrast in value with foundation.
   Strip cut to save time.
   Layer 4 fabrics.
   Cut strips the depth of petals.
   Use template and rotary cutter to cut petals.

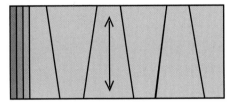
Cutting petals from strips

• Center
   cut one or cut a 10" square and texture fabric with elastic thread. (Please see page 155.)

To create pointed petals: Fold petals in half lengthwise, right sides together. Chain sew across straight ends. Clip petals apart and trim fabric at fold. (This reduces the bulk in the point.) Finger press seam allowance open. Turn end into finished position. Use a point turner to form sharp point. Press. Use a little spray starch for crisp edge.

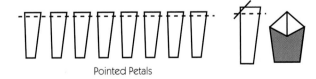
Pointed Petals

To create rounded petals: Fold over 1" of petal tip, right sides together. Mark curved stitching line on fold over using the curved pressing template as

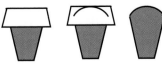
Rounded Petals

a guide. Sew on marked curve line. Trim curve to ⅛". Clip to seam line. Turn carefully forming smooth curve. Press well over pressing template, rolling seam line slightly to back. Use a little spray starch to keep curved edge crisp.

To sew Dresden Plate: Sew two petals, right sides together. Start ⅛" from top edge to avoid creating thread whiskers.
   • Backstitch to fold.
   • Reverse stitching direction.
   • Sew to end of petal.
Join into pairs, then ¼ circles. Join to form circle. Press seams to one side. Dresden plate should lay flat.

Sew

HINT
If plate does not lay flat, check for uneven seam allowances. Slight adjustments may have to be made in a few seam allowances. If so, make adjustments on petals opposite each other to keep plate balanced.

Centering Dresden Plate on foundation: Mark foundation diagonals with fabric marking pen or light creases with the iron. Four plate points will touch lines and center plate. Remove markings or crease lines. Place plate and foundation on batting and backing.

Appliqué Dresden Plate: Decide on type of stitch that will work with your machine. Always test stitch on scrap of fabric before appliquéing. Quilt and appliqué at the same time by stitching through all layers.

Apply center of Dresden Plate: Cut center using cutting template. Run a gathering stitch (about 6 stitches/inch).

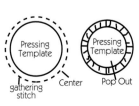
Pressing Template   Pressing Template
gathering stitch   Center   Pop Out

Place pressing template on center:
- Pull up gathers over template.
- Press edge using a little spray starch.
- Pop pressing template from center.

Use invisible thread and blind hem stitch to secure center to Dresden Plate.

Quilt: Stitch in the seam line between petals. Outline quilt ¼" from outside of petals, if desired.

GRANDMOTHER'S FAN

Granny's Fan is similar to the Dresden Plate in many ways. It is made with sewn blades which are appliquéd to a foundation. The fan looks most natural when it is pieced in light and contrasting dark fabrics to represent the angles of a fan. The reverse or backside of a fabric often works very well to achieve the shadowed effect.

Grandmother's Fan

PAPER FOLDED TEMPLATES

Fan: Draw ¼ circle, 10" radius.
Fan Base: Use same center, draw 4" arc.
Isolate fan and arc sections.

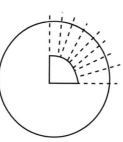

Fan:
- Fold ¼ circle into 8 equal sections.
- Isolate one section.
- Add ¼" seam allowance.

Fan Base:
- Add seam allowance to ¼ circle.

Fabrics:
- Cut 4 light wedges.
- Cut 4 dark wedges.
- Cut 1 fan base.

Foundation fabric: 13" square

Construction:

Sew fan wedges together, alternating light and dark fabrics. Press seams to one side. Finish top by adding lace or other trim to upper edge of fan, right sides together. Turn trim to finished position.

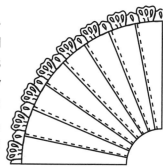

Lay fan base on lower edge of fan:
- Have right sides together.
- Match centers of fan and base.
- Pin.
- Match straight sides of fan and base.
- Pin.
- Sew curved edge, arranging fabrics as you sew.

(You can do it! It is like putting in a sleeve.)

Make a quilt sandwich: backing, batting, foundation.

Position fan:

Position completed fan in lower corner of foundation. Stitch in the seam line next to lace. Quilt in the seam line between wedges.

Quilting Design:

Transfer bow design to foundation. Stitch around design.

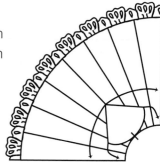

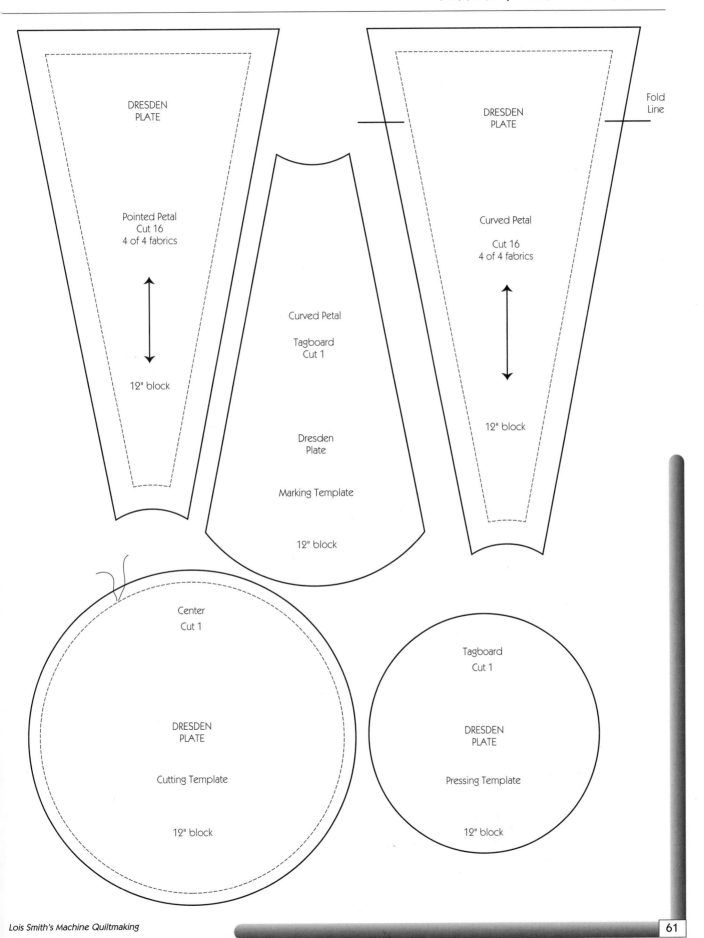

DRESDEN
PLATE

Pointed Petal
Cut 16
4 of 4 fabrics

12" block

DRESDEN
PLATE

Fold
Line

Curved Petal

Cut 16
4 of 4 fabrics

12" block

Curved Petal

Tagboard
Cut 1

Dresden
Plate

Marking Template

12" block

Center
Cut 1

DRESDEN
PLATE

Cutting Template

12" block

Tagboard
Cut 1

DRESDEN
PLATE

Pressing Template

12" block

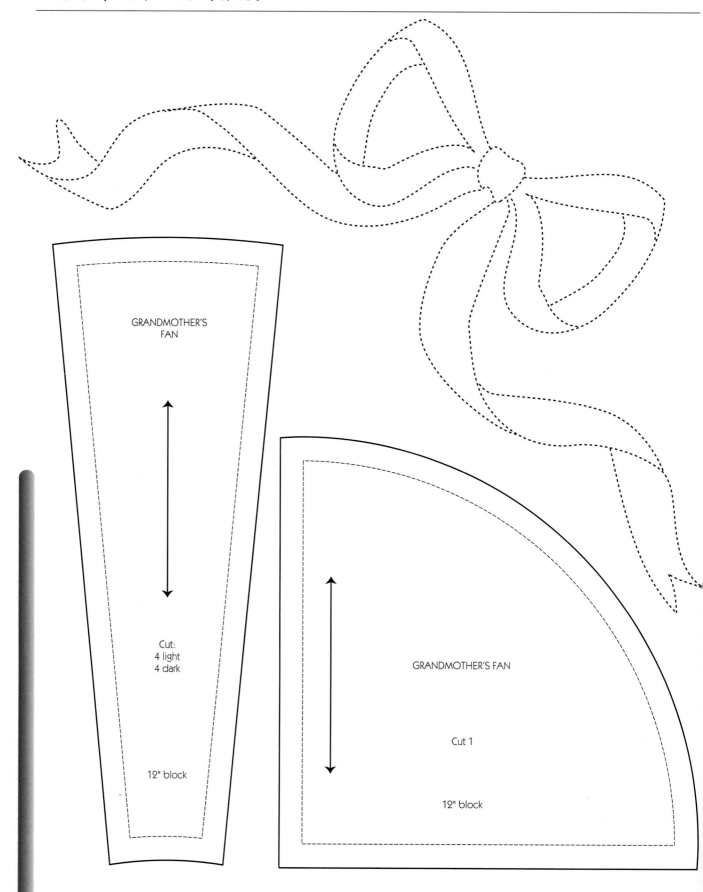

GRANDMOTHER'S
FAN

Cut:
4 light
4 dark

12" block

GRANDMOTHER'S FAN

Cut 1

12" block

LESSON 5
EXPANDING
SKILLS

ALTERNATIVE
DRAFTING METHOD
•
BIAS STRIP
SPEED PIECING
•
FIVE-PATCH BLOCKS
•
PIECING &
APPLIQUÉING
CURVES

Quiltmaking offers exciting challenges along the way. The Five-Patch designs require a new drafting technique. The Clamshell block will be slightly tedious but well worth the effort. Friends will rave over this block but will question you when you affirm that you made it all by machine.

THE FIVE-PATCH DESIGNS

GOALS OF LESSON FIVE
• Make and quilt at least three new blocks
• Continue additional quilting on previous blocks, if desired

SKILLS
• Drafting the Five-Patch grid
• Five-Patch designs
• More speed piecing techniques
• Appliquéd curves
• Pieced curves

The Five-Patch blocks are well balanced as they actually have 25 divisions and a definite center square. These traditional patterns frequently have crossbars separating four rotating corner designs. This subtle sense of motion adds energy as well as aesthetic rhythm to the quilt.

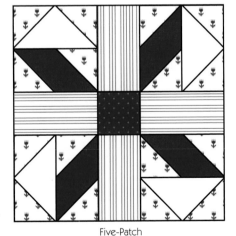
Five-Patch

Since a 12" block does not mathematically divide evenly by five, another method of drafting will be illustrated. By taking the time to understand this method of drafting, you can expand your quiltmaking possibilities. Graph paper will not be used. With this method, any block can be drafted to any given size, even if it is unusual or uneven.

DRAFTING THE FIVE-PATCH

Draw a 12" square.

Ask yourself: What number larger than 12 (size of block) is divisible by 5? (Five-Patch) **Answer:** 15 Place one end of the long ruler in the lower left corner of the 12" square. Place the ruler so that the 15" mark of the ruler touches the right side of the square.

Now ask yourself: Five goes into 15 how many times? **Answer:** 3. Place a dot at the 3", 6", 9", and 12" marks of the ruler on the 12" square. Use a T-square to draw straight lines through the dots from top to bottom of square.

Turn grid a quarter of a turn and repeat. When you have completed drawing the second set of lines, there will be 25 squares. Use these squares to draw the Five-Patch templates.

FIVE-PATCH TEMPLATES

To make Five-Patch templates use a Five-Patch grid of 25 squares. Shade in desired patterns. Trace pattern piece onto graph paper. Add seam allowance. Finish templates.

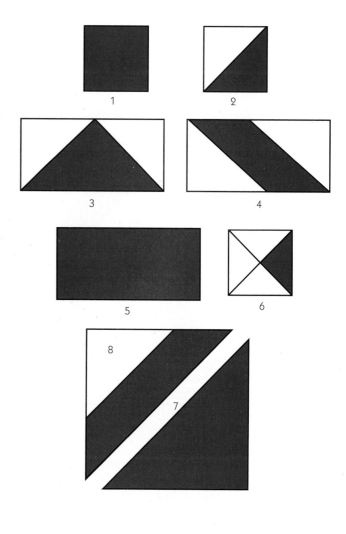

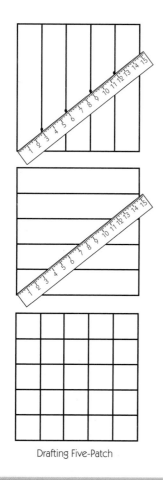

Drafting Five-Patch

RED CROSS

Use four different fabrics for corner squares. Each section rotates a ¼ turn. A crisp secondary design develops when the center triangles are deepest value. A stripe works well for the center cross.

Red Cross

JACK-IN-THE-BOX

Select fabrics that will enhance the design. A fold over design is implied. Use showy fabric for triangle tips. Use muted or shadowed fabric in the connecting arms.

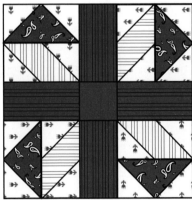

Jack in the Box

CROSS AND CROWNS

Cross and Crowns

Four layers or planes of design can be imagined. Work to achieve depth by careful fabric planning. Light colors advance, dark colors recede. Bright colors advance, muted colors recede.

BIAS STRIP SPEED PIECING

Repetition plays a role in quiltmaking. When the identical shapes and fabrics repeat frequently, speed piecing methods save time and reduce boredom with generally accurate results.

FLYING GEESE

The shape and size of the triangle to be pieced must first be determined. In Flying Geese there are many repeating triangles. These are called half square triangles. The unit is a square made up of two triangles.

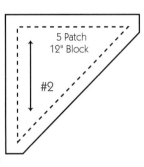

5 Patch 12" Block

#2

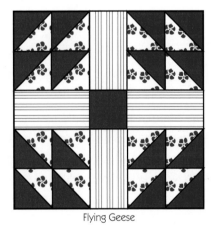

Flying Geese

Two contrasting bias strips will be cut, layered right sides together, and sewn on both long sides. Triangles will be cut from the strip, and they will become squares when pressed open. The depth of the strips is not critical since a template will still be used.

Five-Patch 12" block

#2

measure depth

To determine the width of the bias strips, measure triangle template which includes seam allowance from tip to the center of the longest side. Add an additional ¼". Cut enough bias strips to make 16 triangle combinations.

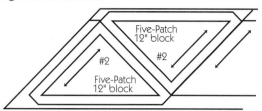

Directions:

Carefully press two bias strips together using spray starch for cohesion. Sew long sides together with ¼" seam allowance. Using your template as a guide, cut desired number of triangle combinations. Carefully open triangle and press seam open creating the finished square. Check fabric square with square template for accuracy. Trim if necessary.

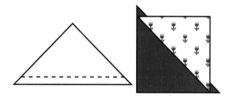

Curves

Curves have long been reserved for the experienced quiltmaker. It is possible to make beautiful curves every time with a little help from your machine and your iron. The appliquéd clamshell design will delight and amaze you and your friends. It will be the attention getter in your quilt with its composite display of color and its striking curved lines. Moon Over the Mountain will introduce the pieced curve. The Drunkard's Path blocks will feature pieced, curved designs which add unusual curvilinear designs to the quilt.

Standards of Good Workmanship
Curves should be smooth and round with no tucks or flat spots. Appliqué stitching should be unobtrusive or decorative.

The Clamshell
The Clamshell block takes about 56 clamshells. Portions of the edge clamshells will be trimmed away. Therefore, start with a set of 15" backing and batting so that you will have a 12" block when you are finished. After the clamshells are prepared, they will be sewn directly to the batting/backing sandwich. No additional quilting will be required.

The Clamshell

Directions:
Cut 56 clamshells. Use all values sparked by a few zingers. Layer fabrics for multiple cutting. Use appliqué (duckbill) scissors, held perpendicular to surface to cut multilayers with accuracy.

Duckbill Scissors

Machine basting clamshells:
Stitch ⅛" from outer curved edge of each clamshell. Use long stitch length, 6 stitches per inch. Use contrasting thread colors in bobbin and needle. (Bobbin thread pulls easiest.) Chain baste leaving 6" between clamshells. Clip apart.

Pressing clamshells:
Make pressing template from lightweight cardboard or heat resistant template plastic. Place

Front   Back

clamshell and pressing template together aligning bottom of clamshell with reference mark on the template. Gather by pulling on bobbin thread. Set crease with spray starch.

HINT

Spray the starch into a small saucer or jar lid, not directly onto fabric. Apply with finger or small brush to folded edge.

Positioning clamshells: Align first row of clamshells, draw a guideline 3" from top of batting. Have touching clamshells stand on this line. Draw more guidelines as necessary.

Appliquéing clamshells: Stitch clamshells in place; use invisible thread; use reduced blind hem stitch; only the grabbing stitch will be going into the clamshell.

Blind Hem Stitch

Lay the next rows of clams in the same manner with pressed curve positioned on seam allowance of previous row. Half clamshells can be used at beginning and ending of rows.

Cut Off

Trim block to 12½". Leave ¼" seam allowance above second row of clamshells. Save scrap for Crazy Patch.

MOON OVER THE MOUNTAIN

This pieced picture block can either be a nighttime scene or an early morning sunrise. Realistic fabrics can be used for the sky or you can actually create your own sunrise or sunset with strip piecing.

Piecing curves may seem awkward at first, but it is really quite simple, requiring a positive attitude, and very little pinning. Find the centers of corresponding

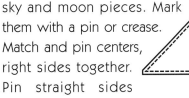

sky and moon pieces. Mark them with a pin or crease. Match and pin centers, right sides together. Pin straight sides together near future seam line. Align raw edges with your fingers. Sew to center. Stop with needle in fabric. Rearrange fabric and continue to other straight side. Press fabrics toward moon to add a slight textural relief.

Joining quarters: Sew two quarters of block together. Sew the two halves together.

Joining Quarters

FANCY ALTERNATIVE

String pieced sky: Cut three sky pieces from muslin, adding ¼" beyond seam allowance for "squirm room." Mark directional ray lines on muslin.

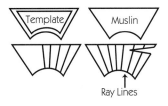

Template   Muslin

Ray Lines

Moon Over the Mountain

Use irregular string quilting techniques (1½" strings) to fill up muslin sky. Start string quilting in the center of each muslin piece. Use directional lines to align sewing side of strip. Trim excess fabric from bottom strips as sky develops. Cut again using the sky template.

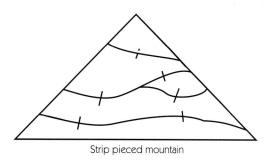

Strip pieced mountain

Curved, strip-pieced mountain: Cut mountain shape from freezer paper. Draw desired mountain segments on freezer paper. Mark reference points for joining. Cut apart on drawn lines. Iron segments on desired fabrics. Cut out segments adding ¼" seam allowance on all sides. Match reference points and sew segments together. Check size and shape with original template. Sew block together.

DRUNKARD'S PATH

Drunkard's Path is a block based on two templates. When pieced, the contrasting fabric values create a pattern with unusual twists and turns.

Pattern drafting: The basic unit of this Four-Patch design is a 3" square. An arc divides the block. Draw an arc with a radius of 2". Isolate two sections and add seam allowances to each piece.

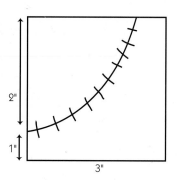

Fabrics: Contrasting values work well. Cut eight light from each template. Cut eight dark from each template.

Positioning: Fold curved edges in half to determine midpoints. Pin midpoints of curves together. Pin straight edges together near seam line to properly align for sewing.

Sewing: Sew to midpoint pin. Rearrange fabrics without removing from machine. Finish sewing to end. Check to see if curve is round and smooth: rip out any poorly-sewn areas; sew again. Press seams in either direction. Do not press seams open. Sew design together.

HINT
A light and a dark fabric should be used for the Drunkard's Path.

VARIATION ON THE DRUNKARD'S PATH BLOCK

Two templates create these curved Four-Patch designs based on variation of the Drunkard's Path. Alternated arrangements of the pieced squares produce a wide variety of blocks.

Drunkard's Path

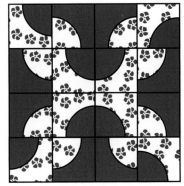

Fallen Timbers

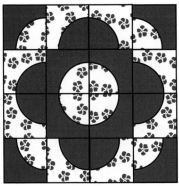

Love Ring

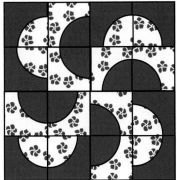

Carolyn's Path

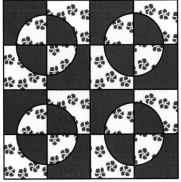

Snowball

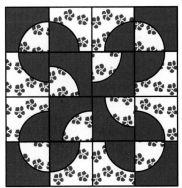

Fool's Puzzle I

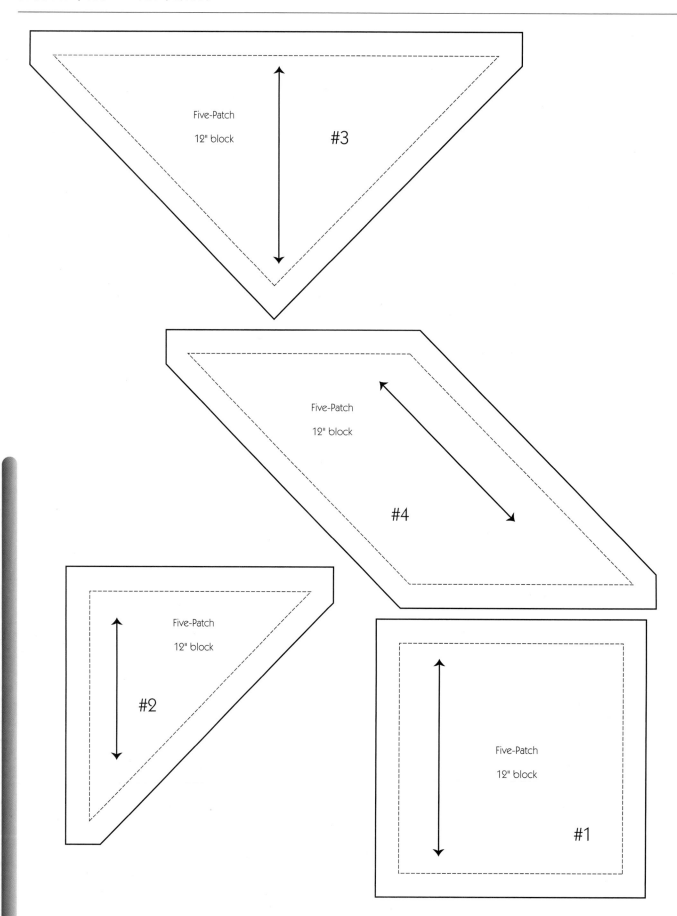

Five-Patch

12" block

#3

Five-Patch

12" block

#4

Five-Patch

12" block

#2

Five-Patch

12" block

#1

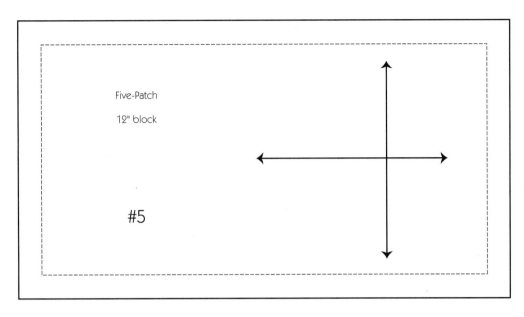

Five-Patch

12" block

#5

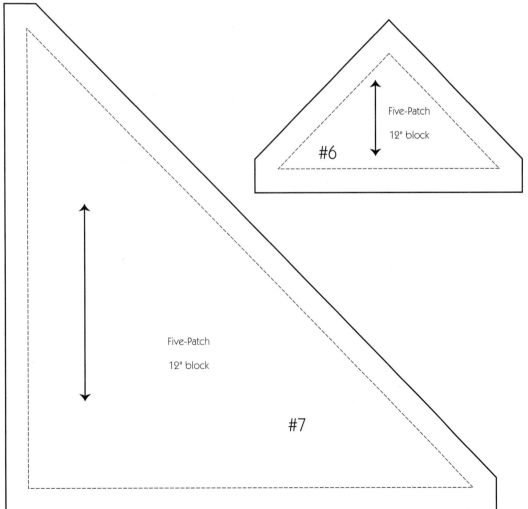

Five-Patch

12" block

#6

Five-Patch

12" block

#7

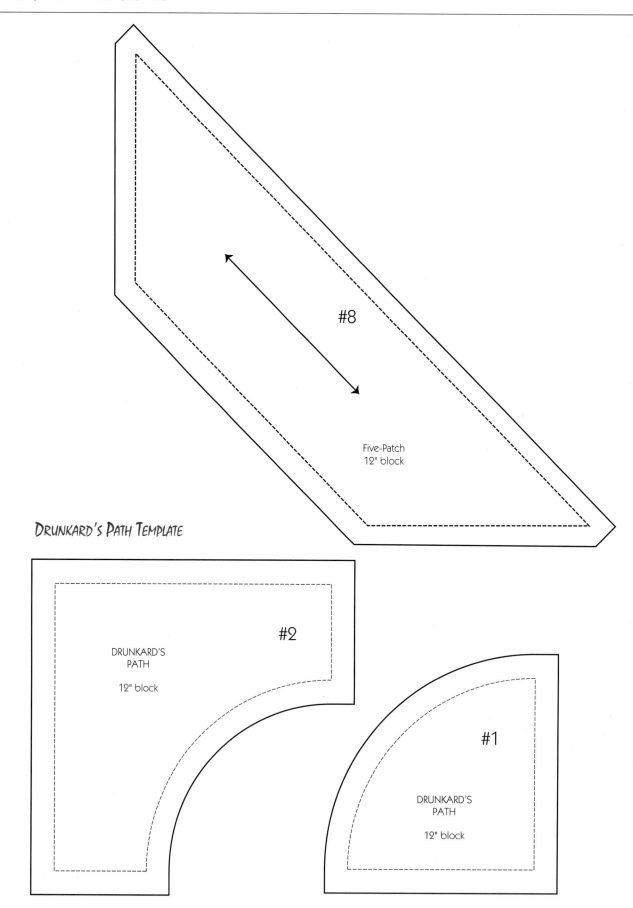

#8

Five-Patch
12" block

DRUNKARD'S PATH TEMPLATE

#2

DRUNKARD'S
PATH

12" block

#1

DRUNKARD'S
PATH

12" block

CLAMSHELL TEMPLATE

Use compass and graph paper. Draw and quarter a 3" circle. Connect side and base marks with same arc. Add ¼" seam allowance on all sides.

CLAMSHELL PRESSING TEMPLATE

Draw 3" Clamshell. Do not add seam allowances. Add a handle to hold onto when pressing.

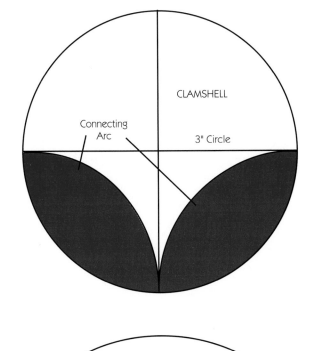

CLAMSHELL

Connecting Arc

3" Circle

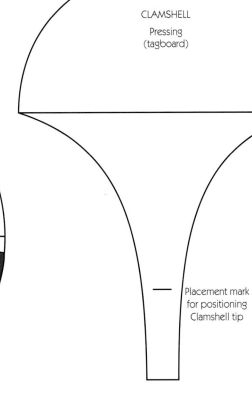

CLAMSHELL
Pressing
(tagboard)

Placement mark for positioning Clamshell tip

Seam Allowance

CLAMSHELL

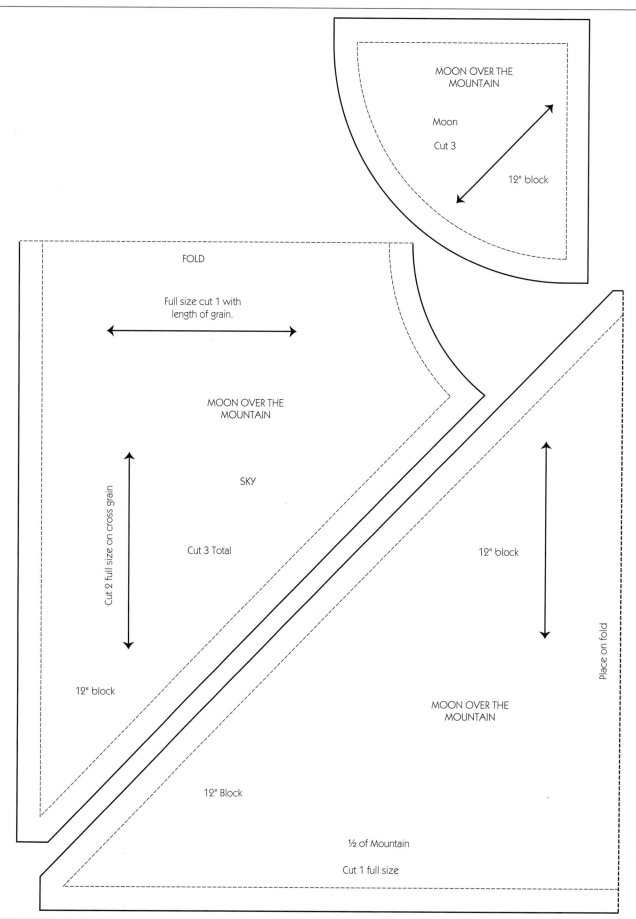

MOON OVER THE
MOUNTAIN

Moon

Cut 3

12" block

FOLD

Full size cut 1 with
length of grain.

MOON OVER THE
MOUNTAIN

SKY

Cut 3 Total

Cut 2 full size on cross grain

12" block

12" block

Place on fold

MOON OVER THE
MOUNTAIN

12" Block

½ of Mountain

Cut 1 full size

MAKING A SAMPLER QUILT

You have the power to make your quilt exceptional. Take the time to look at your collection of blocks. What else would you like to see in your quilt? Enjoy the process of making your last few blocks. Have you noticed how your skill level has increased?

BLOCKS WITH SPECIAL MEANING

GOALS OF LESSON SIX
- Critique your blocks
- Personalize your quilt with blocks of interest
- Make three or more blocks
- Think about visual balance

SKILLS
- Additional appliqué techniques
- Photographs on fabric

CRITIQUE

These are the final blocks to be made for the quilt. Take time to critique what you have made. The blocks themselves as well as the colors and the values needed to visually balance the quilt should be evaluated while there is still time to make modifications. Ask the opinion of a friend or a child.

Does one fabric jump out at you? Add more of it in the remaining blocks and watch it settle down.

Do you need a spark of interest? Possibly you have overused your original zinger, and it no longer provides that dash of unexpected surprise. Try adding a sharper, more workable zinger in small amounts.

Is your quilt a little dull? Try extending the depth of your palette with a deeper value or add a little pep and energy with a touch of yellow or orange.

Are some of your first blocks less than perfect? Love them! Use them. How great that your skills are improving!

Does your quilt seem a little impersonal? By all means, make some picture blocks. They can be appliquéd or pieced.

EXPANDING APPLIQUÉ TECHNIQUES

Appliqué enables you to make fabric pictures. Blocks can be original designs or patterns that have special meaning for you. Design ideas can come from almost anywhere including photographs or postcards. Cutting shapes freehand often yields great, simple, easy to appliqué designs.

Elements appliquéd in traditional quilts generally have an edge that is turned under in some manner and stitched in place with either an invisible blind hem stitch or a decorative stitch. The edge can be finished by either turning under ¼" or by creating a faced shape, two like shapes sewn together and turned. Edges that are covered by another do not need to be turned under since they will be hidden by subsequent design pieces.

KEEP IT SIMPLE

Simple shapes work best for appliqué. Fine details can be added with stitching, inking or embellishments. Ultra-Suede® designs can be cut without seam allowances and secured with a blind hem stitch and invisible thread to create details too small to execute easily by traditional methods.

A combination of piecing and appliqué may be used in some blocks where the background is first constructed and then completed with appliqué designs.

The size and the complexity of the appliqué pieces often dictates which appliqué method will be most appropriate for any given design piece. The template materials will vary also. All templates will be cut without seam allowances. They will be added to the actual fabric when the shape is cut.

Appliqué Method 1. Cutting/pressing templates (use for fairly large pieces and simple shapes): Cut templates from lightweight cardboard (file folders) or

Template

heat resistant template plastic without seam allowance. Add seam allowance to fabric by eye-balling the ¼". Templates will serve as patterns and also as pressing templates. Gather edges of circles and tight curves using long gathering stitch. Place template on fabric and pull gathering stitches to shape. Press straight on fabric over sides of template.

Appliqué Method 2. Faced shapes (for small pieces and irregularly shaped edges): Cut templates out of freezer paper. Fabrics will be layered right sides together. Iron templates to fabric back. Stitch, following template contour.

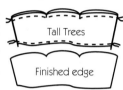

Tall Trees

Finished edge

Cut shapes adding ¼" seam allowance. Clip curves. Turn right side out.

Use point turner to smooth edge:
- Work edge so seam does not show on top.
- Use starch to hold crisp edge.
- Trim away back fabric, if desired.

If a piece is sewn on all sides, slit back to turn.

Appliqué Method 3. Double freezer paper templates (an alternative freezer paper method of appliqué): Cut duplicate freezer paper templates. Iron template to back of fabric. Glue the second template to the back of the first, dull side to

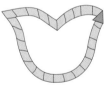

dull side. Cut fabric adding ¼" seam allowance. Press fabric edges onto shiny side.
- Freezer paper will hold edges.
- Clip curves if necessary.
- For sharp corners fold corner tip first.

Remove freezer paper before applying to base.

Or finish appliqué block:
- Cut away area behind appliqué.
- Remove freezer paper.

Appliqué basics

Cut a 13" background square to allow for squirm room. Lay appliqué pieces on background. Plan a sewing strategy. Start with back pieces first. Stitch with a blind hem or decorative stitch. Trim block to desired size.

Machine set-up:
- #9 Jeans needle
- regular presser foot
- blind hem stitch
- stitch length 1½"
- zigzag width 1½ or less
- invisible thread in needle
- bobbin to match backing
- slightly lowered top tension
- Test stitches on sample

STANDARDS OF GOOD WORKMANSHIP (APPLIQUÉ)
- Design should flow smoothly.
- Curves should be smooth and free from puckers.
- Points should be sharp.
- Stitches should be small and hold appliqué securely.
- Thread should match appliqué unless decorative stitching is used.
- Grain line should be visually pleasing.
- Appliqué edges should be secure with no raw edges exposed.
- Similar pieces should be equal in size.

ASSATEAGUE LIGHTHOUSE, VIRGINIA 1833

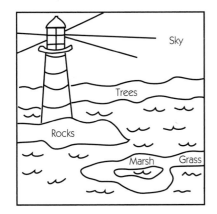

Seam sky and water. Make lighthouse (method 1). Press pieced lighthouse over lighthouse template. Use starch to hold edges.

Make templates A, B, C from freezer paper (method 2). Join sections of A1 to A to make one template. Create faced trees, rocks, marsh grass. Lay small facing piece on right side of marsh grass where water will show through. Stitch on marked line. Trim facing close to stitching. Clip remaining seam allowance. Completely pull facing to back. (You have created a hole.)

Position appliqué pieces. Blind hem stitch around pieces and around the hole.

Add details:
- Place deli wrap paper or other stabilizer behind stitching areas.
- Satin stitch windows.
- Blindstitch Ultra-Suede® lighthouse cap and observation deck.
- Use machine stitching for details in light area.

HEARTS AND FLOWERS APPLIQUÉ
Very simple shapes can be visually pleasing. Strive to have all repeating shapes identically sized and aligned symmetrically on the background. The center circle should be perfectly round. The center pictured is a dime-size circle.

Hearts and Flowers

Use method 3 for flowers and leaves. Use method 2 to make faced hearts. Make a dime-size circle. Fold a 1" strip into quarters to create ¼" stem.

Align design pieces on the diagonal axis. Blindstitch.

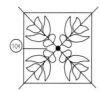

PIECED PICTURE BLOCKS

Pieced picture blocks are geometric. They can be embellished with appliqué and other enhancing details. Preplanning will allow the appliquéd edges to be included in the seam allowances between the pieces of the block.

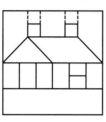

House on a Hill

HOUSE ON A HILL

Piece a traditional house with the templates given or draft your own pattern and create a house or townhouse that looks like yours. Include your shutters, house number, sidewalk, and identifying greenery. Search for architectural fabrics in the proper scale for the roof and siding.

THE SAILBOAT

Use Four-Patch templates.

Water can be cut in one piece (3½" x 12½").

Special touches:
- lace can be inserted to resemble ocean.
- quilt ocean waves, wind, sun rays, etc.

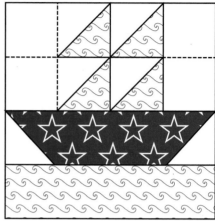

Sailboat

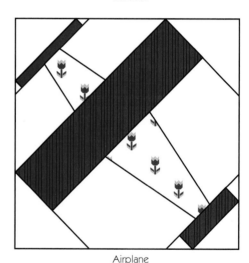

Airplane

ORIGINAL DESIGNS

Vacation memories can be captured and included in a quilt. Designing and drafting your own patterns from postcard ideas or photographs is personally meaningful and extremely satisfying.

Patterns can be drafted on freezer paper. Some quilt shops sell freezer paper with ¼" graph to make the job even easier. After the design is drafted to your liking, the pieces can be cut apart and used as templates. Accurate seam allowances will be added as you cut each piece.

ROSEVILLE BRIDGE, 1910

This block was designed from a vacation postcard picturing the bridge that crosses Big Raccoon Creek at Coxville, Indiana. The bridge was built in 1910 and is 263' long and 16' wide. Templates developed from the postcard are provided.

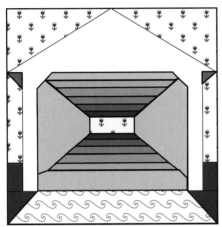

Roseville Bridge, 1910

Piece inside of bridge. Join four inside bridge pieces to end of bridge (sky fabric) matching reference dots.

Sew to dots, leaving seam allowances free. Replace upper corners of inner bridge with small triangles.

Piece segments. Finish piecing block. This is a combination block using both a Four-Patch and Nine-Patch grid.

PHOTOGRAPHS AND PICTURES IN QUILTS

The idea of using photographs and pictures in quilts is not new. But the use of modern technology to facilitate the process and to add color images is new and constantly changing.

Favorite Christmas recipes from three generations are included in a special recipe block.

The original recipe cards were taken to a copy shop and transferred onto fabric while I waited.

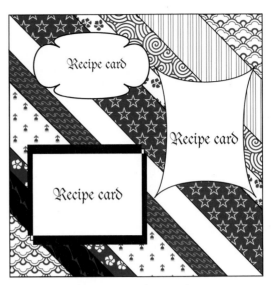

The recipe cards were not harmed.

When time is a big factor, copy shops that also transfer images to T-shirts are the answer. They have the technology to transfer the photo image to fabric without reversing the image or distorting the color. Satisfactory results are guaranteed in a few minutes. (Please see resources in appendix.)

Home computers and copy machines can also convert text and pictures to fabrics. Informative labels as well as photographs (black-and-white or color) can be included in your quilts with little effort. Newspaper clippings, certificates of award, or even birth announcements might add just the appropriate touch.

Directions:
Iron a 9" by 12" piece of freezer paper to the back of white or desired fabric. With rotary cutter, trim to 8½" by 11". Cautiously feed through printer or copy machine. (See printer manual for instructions.) Spray lightly with clear acrylic spray for permanency.

THE TIME CAPSULE OR CRAZY PATCH

The Time Capsule is the contemporary crazy patch. Here is another place to leave a note...and a picture! What were the major events of the year for you? Did you add a new family member, get a new car, move to a new home? All of these events can be pictorially recorded along with fancy stitches on your fabric scraps. What might seem silly as you stitch will become treasured in just a short time.

The Time Capsule is an original design and there is no pattern. You will be sewing down bits and pieces of fabric and other mementos and pictures.

Directions:
Use a 15" backing and batting. Sew scraps, laces, photos directly to batting. Press edges under and appliqué and/or stitch and flip using the string quilting technique. Quilt using decorative machine stitches. Trim block to 12½".

Crazy Patch

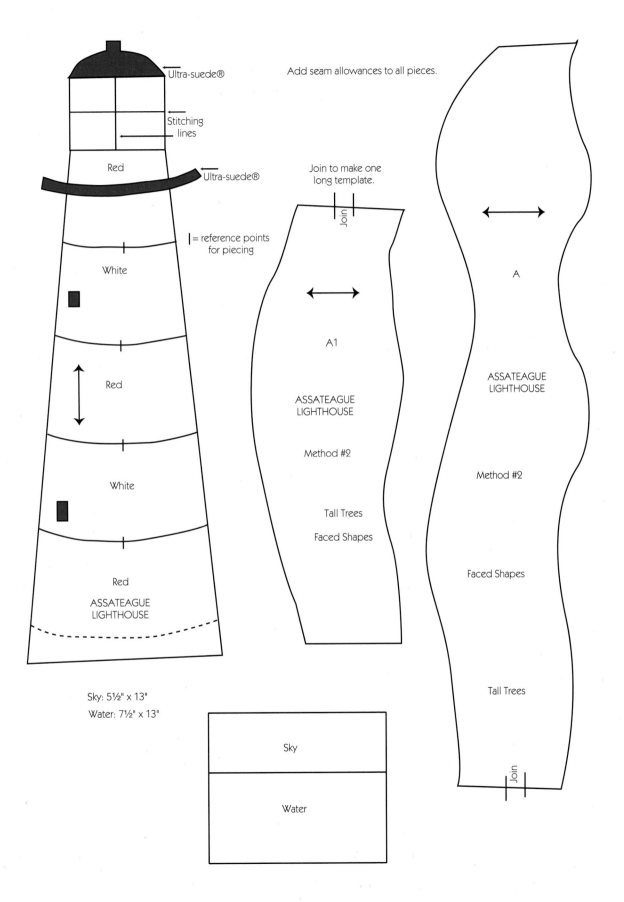

Ultra-suede®

Stitching
lines

Red

Ultra-suede®

| = reference points
for piecing

White

Red

White

Red

ASSATEAGUE
LIGHTHOUSE

Sky: 5½" x 13"
Water: 7½" x 13"

Add seam allowances to all pieces.

Join to make one
long template.

Join

A1

ASSATEAGUE
LIGHTHOUSE

Method #2

Tall Trees

Faced Shapes

A

ASSATEAGUE
LIGHTHOUSE

Method #2

Faced Shapes

Tall Trees

Join

Sky

Water

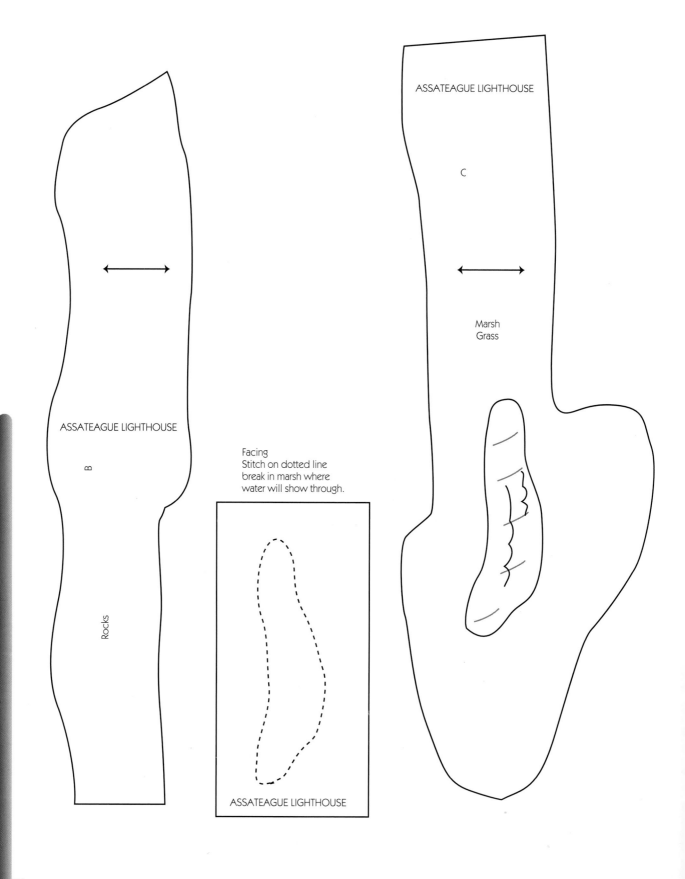

ASSATEAGUE LIGHTHOUSE

C

Marsh
Grass

ASSATEAGUE LIGHTHOUSE

B

Rocks

Facing
Stitch on dotted line
break in marsh where
water will show through.

ASSATEAGUE LIGHTHOUSE

HEARTS AND FLOWERS APPLIQUÉ

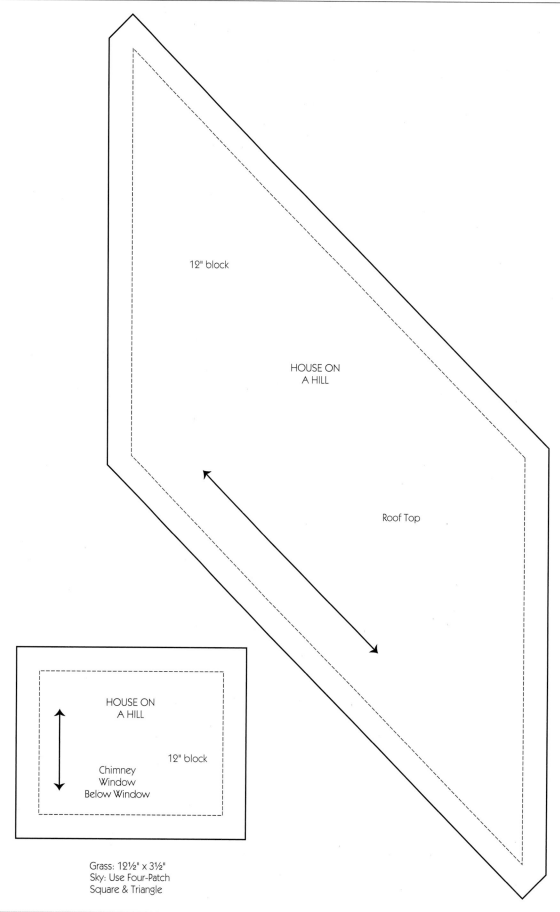

12" block

HOUSE ON
A HILL

Roof Top

HOUSE ON
A HILL

12" block

Chimney
Window
Below Window

Grass: 12½" x 3½"
Sky: Use Four-Patch
Square & Triangle

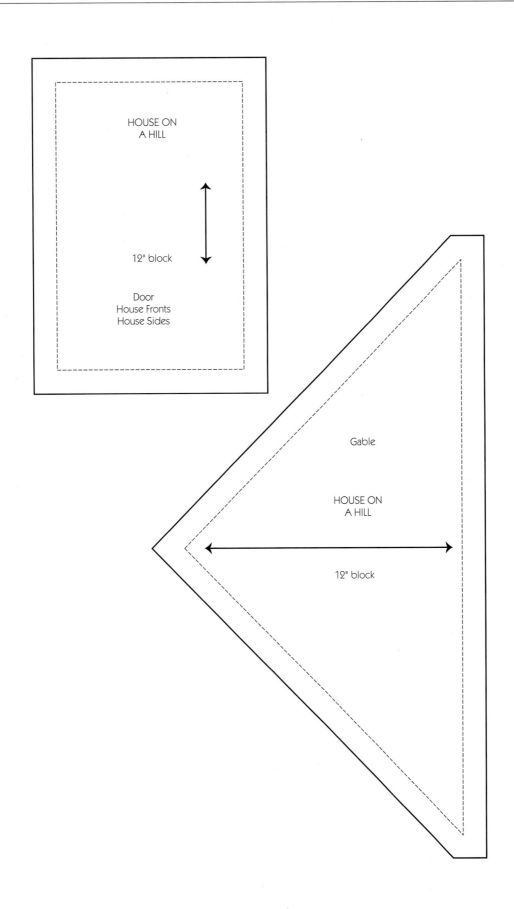

HOUSE ON
A HILL

12" block

Door
House Fronts
House Sides

Gable

HOUSE ON
A HILL

12" block

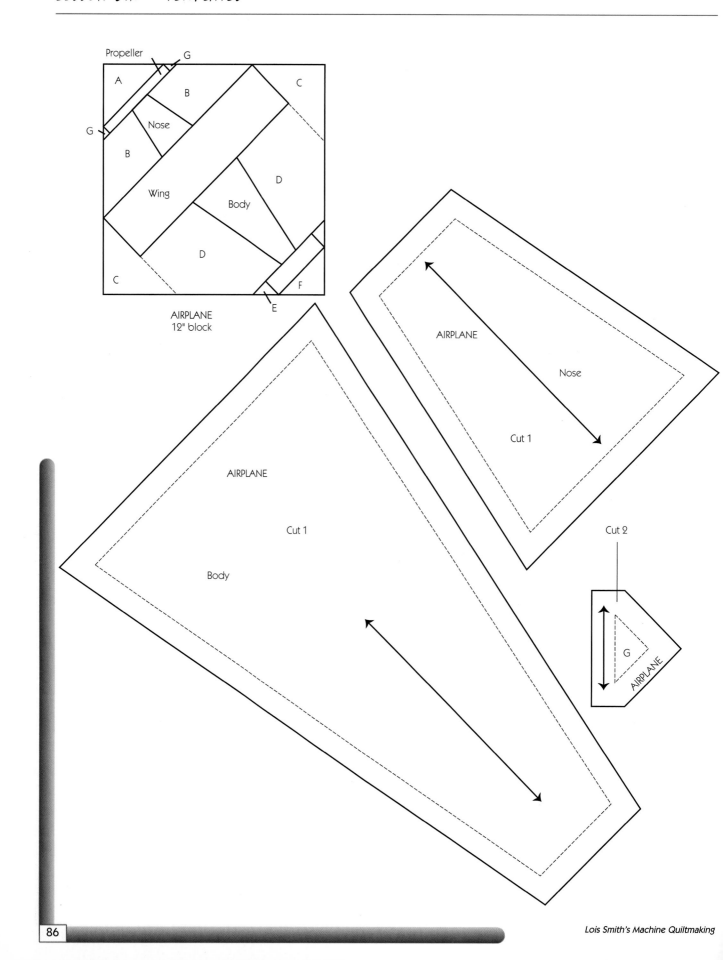

AIRPLANE
12" block

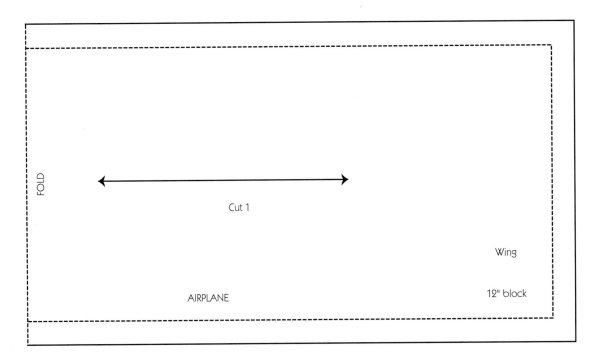

FOLD

← Cut 1 →

Wing

AIRPLANE

12" block

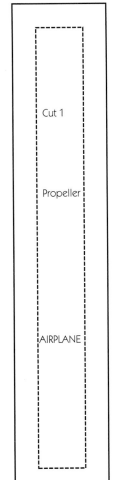

Cut 1

Propeller

AIRPLANE

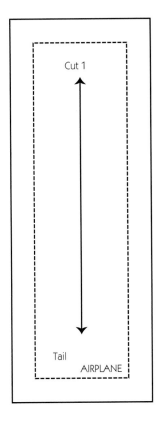

Cut 1

Tail

AIRPLANE

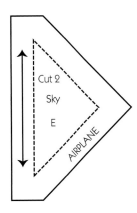

Cut 2

Sky

E

AIRPLANE

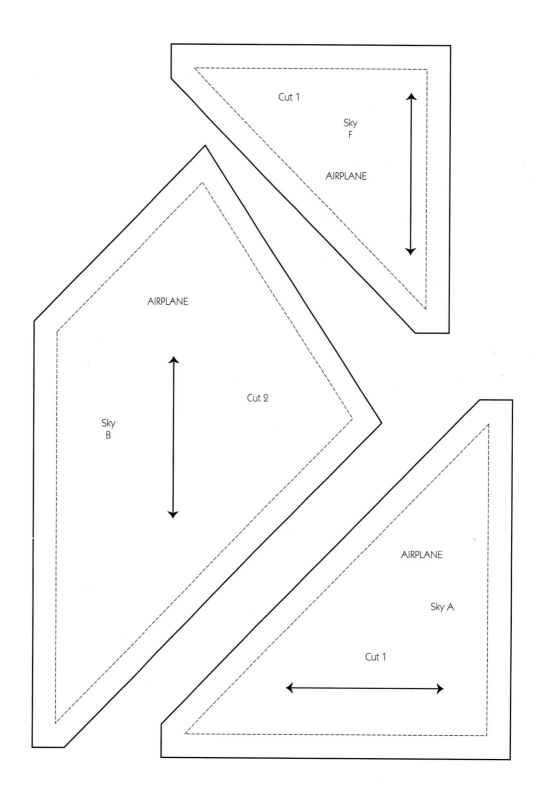

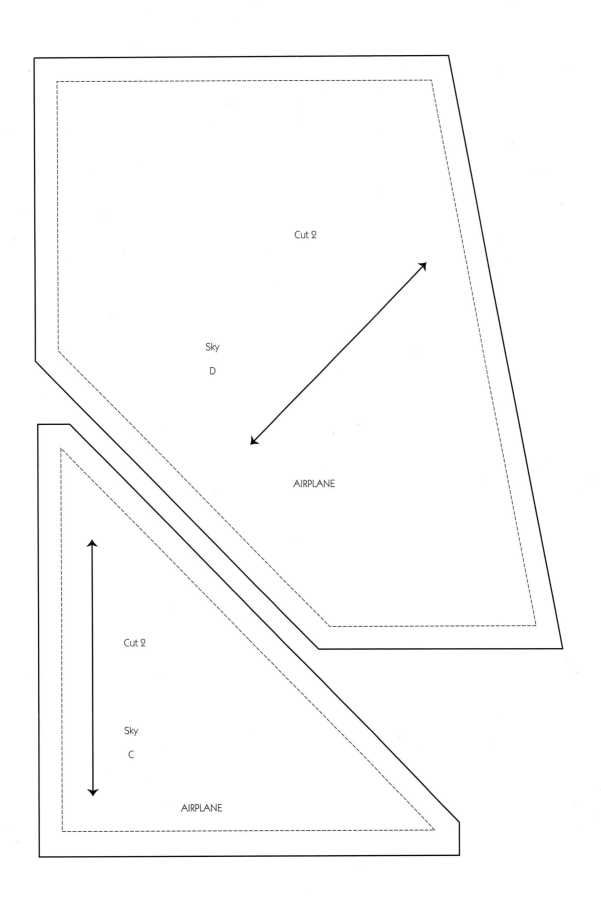

Cut 2

Sky

D

AIRPLANE

Cut 2

Sky

C

AIRPLANE

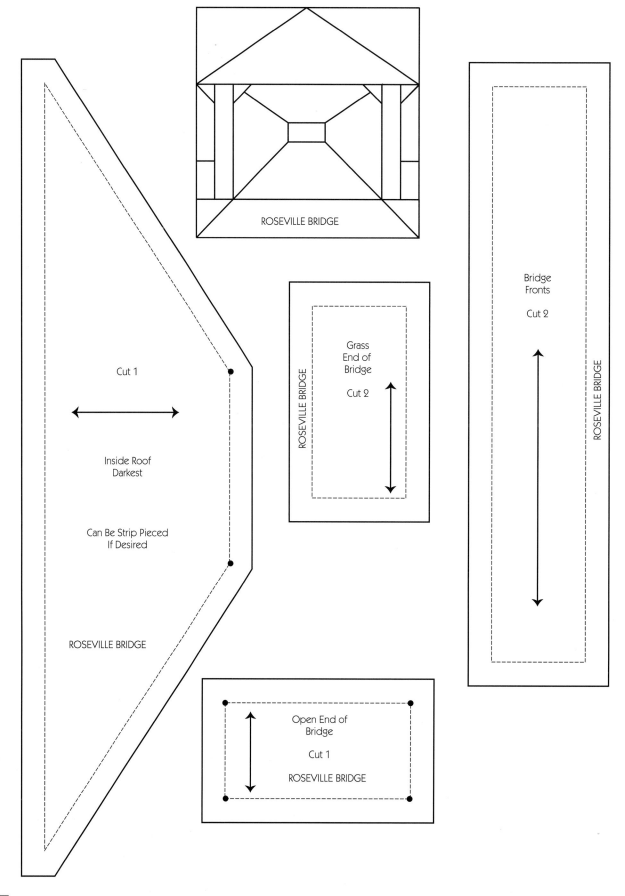

ROSEVILLE BRIDGE

Cut 1

Inside Roof
Darkest

Can Be Strip Pieced
If Desired

ROSEVILLE BRIDGE

ROSEVILLE BRIDGE

Grass
End of
Bridge

Cut 2

Bridge
Fronts

Cut 2

ROSEVILLE BRIDGE

Open End of
Bridge

Cut 1

ROSEVILLE BRIDGE

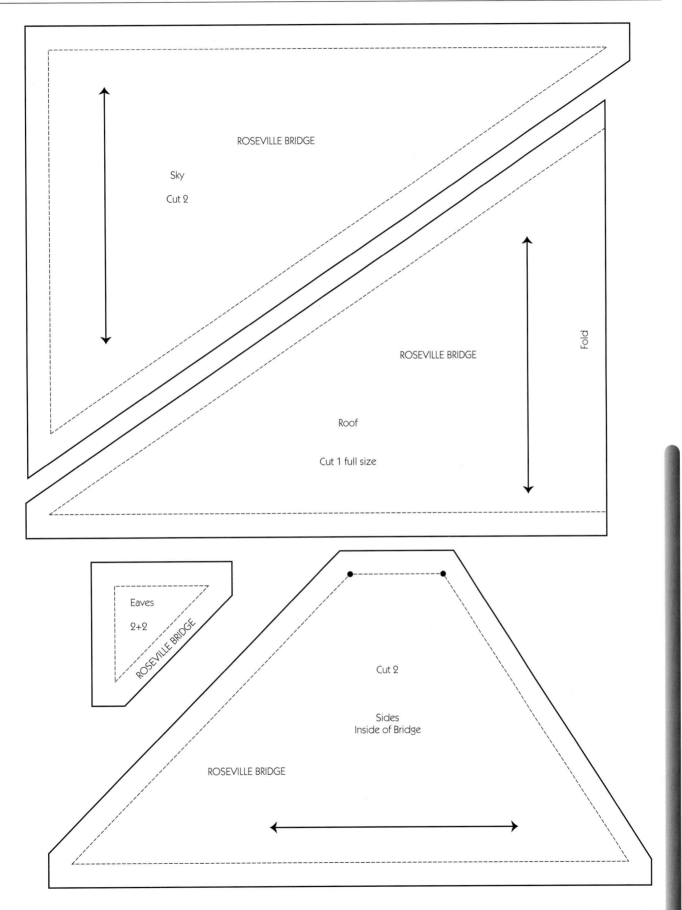

ROSEVILLE BRIDGE

Sky

Cut 2

ROSEVILLE BRIDGE

Roof

Cut 1 full size

Fold

Eaves

2+2

ROSEVILLE BRIDGE

Cut 2

Sides
Inside of Bridge

ROSEVILLE BRIDGE

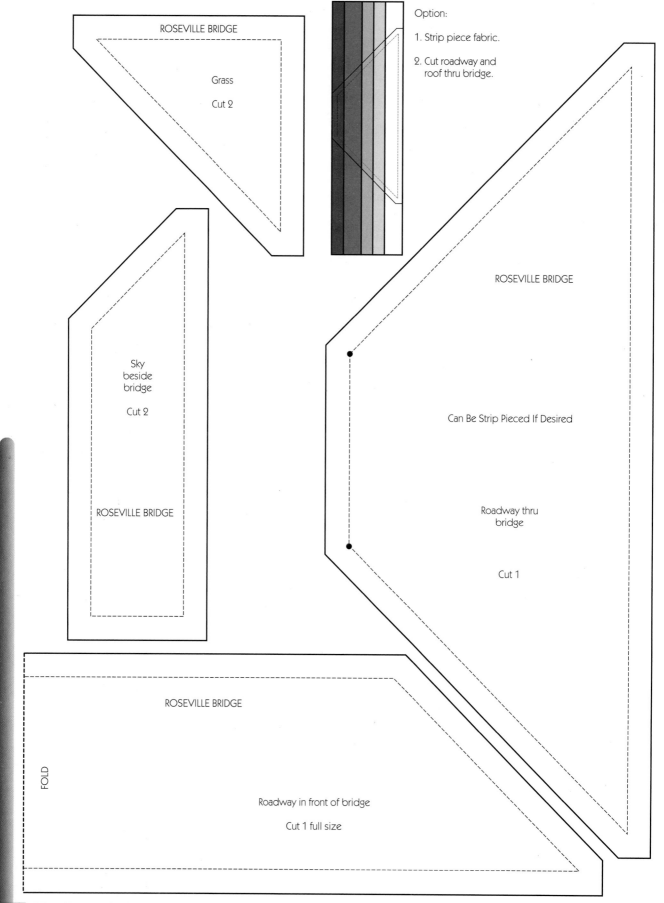

ROSEVILLE BRIDGE

Grass

Cut 2

Option:

1. Strip piece fabric.

2. Cut roadway and roof thru bridge.

ROSEVILLE BRIDGE

Can Be Strip Pieced If Desired

Roadway thru bridge

Cut 1

Sky beside bridge

Cut 2

ROSEVILLE BRIDGE

ROSEVILLE BRIDGE

FOLD

Roadway in front of bridge

Cut 1 full size

T he blocks are finished, and it is time to make a quilt out of your objet d'art. The finishing steps of joining the quilt blocks are as important as the making of the blocks. The process is a little more left brain than the creative experiences you have had with the blocks so far. With this simple method, the finishing will go quickly, and you will be pleased with the results. Please take time to read through these last two chapters to get an overview of the finishing process. Understand the importance of blocks that are of equal size and why measurements should be accurate, written down, and used as a reference.

FROM BLOCKS TO QUILT CORE

GOAL OF LESSON SEVEN
• To finish quilt core

SKILLS
• Balancing block attributes
• Selecting sashing fabric
• Mock string sashing
• Joining blocks into columns
• Blind hem stitch for finishing back
• Considering cornerstones
• Making and adding vertical sashing
• Edge finishes

Make a diagram of your quilt and keep a figures chart.

Figures chart:
Draw squares to represent blocks.
Add sashing (and borders, if any).
Personal block size including seam allowance *
Personal block size sewn into quilt *
Quilt length
Quilt width
Border length
Border width
*Please see sizing the blocks.

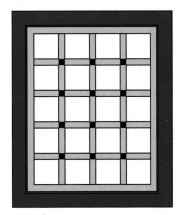

Make notation on the chart as you progress. Quilt finishing does involve simple but accurate calculations. Check and double check figures.

SIZING THE BLOCKS

While it is acceptable for people to be all shapes and sizes, quilt blocks should be uniform in size. A ¼" variance is acceptable, but more than that will cause problems somewhere down the line.

Please sort your blocks into two piles. In the first stack, place the String Quilting, Clamshell, Time Capsule, Log Cabin, Drunkard's Path, and any others that could be trimmed slightly, if necessary, without causing any great harm.

Include in the second group blocks that have definite points that you would choose not to trim. Ohio Star, Jacob's Ladder, Anvil, Jack-in-the-Box all fit into this category.

Measure all blocks from edge to edge. Write down the measurement of each block. Find a common denominator and call this your personal number. For example:

12½" x 12½"	1 block	OK
12¼" x 12¼"	9 blocks	OK
12¼" x 12"	1 block	
12" x 12"	1 block	

Your **personal number** would be 12¼"

The block that is ¼" too large can be eased in without trimming generally. A block that is short on one side can be brought to size by adding a little patch on the short side with matching fabric. Any block that is ¼" or more less than desired will need a small border on all sides: there should be enough backing and batting available.

- Add border strips that are at least 1".
- Press border strips into final position.
- Trim block to personal number (12¼").

Now trim blocks in the first pile using the personal number. Do not rush this process! If points are already missing or have to be trimmed off because the block is way too large, don't panic. When a single block is examined, details seem extremely important. This is a quilt you are making, not just a pile of individual blocks. When everything is sewn together, the beauty of the quilt will not be marred by a cutoff point or two.

FROM BLOCKS TO QUILT: THE TRANSFORMATION

The final placement of the blocks in the quilt will be determined by visual weight, color, value, and design.

Iris by Kathy Samone

Log Cabin, String Quilting, Crazy Patch, and Clamshell appear to be visually heavier than the other designs. Placing these blocks in the corners, over the pillow area, or in the center of the quilt, will distribute the weight.

Scatter bright colors and your zinger fabric throughout the quilt. Also be mindful of curved lines vs. straight lines, and alternate them across the surface.

Blocks should be arranged to maintain a focus in the center of the quilt. Put your best blocks there. Use blocks with diagonal lines to direct the eye to the center.

Study your blocks for a day or two after you think you have the final arrangement. If you haven't found a spot for a design wall, pin them to a curtain or lay them on the floor. Look at them and then let them rest awhile. A fresh look may give you a different perspective. Once you are satisfied, label each block to keep them in order while adding the sashing.

SELECTING THE SASHING

The sashing unifies the disparate quilt blocks and establishes the color of the quilt. A quilt with blue sashing will be seen as a blue quilt even if the blocks are predominantly tan and rust.

Choose a good quality fabric that goes well with your blocks. Almost any quiet print will be a good choice if the color goes well. Avoid plaids and stripes for this mock string method of sashing.

> ### HINT
> Take the finished blocks to the quilt shop at a time when the shop may not be too busy. Look around for a fabric that appeals to you. Let the salespeople offer suggestions also. Spread the blocks out on several different fabrics. Choose the one that you like the best.

MOCK STRING SASHING

Wouldn't it be terrible to love making the blocks and then hate the process of putting them together? Maybe the quilt would never get finished. No, that will not happen.

This quick and easy sashing method will speed you along the way and you will be wearing the badge of quiltmaker in no time. The point of all this stitching is to finish a quilt.

Mock string sashing rapidly transforms the sampler blocks into a great quilt. The mock string sashing is created by folding a long sashing strip in half lengthwise and then stitching ¼" from the fold through the strip, batting, and the backing. When the strip is opened up...voila! The sashing will be completed and ready to cut into the betweens which will attach to the quilt blocks.

The simplicity of this unmarked sashing complements the busy designs of the blocks. The advantage of this method is the speed in which many betweens can be cut from each long strip. In addition, the stitching line holds everything together and also creates the quilting line which will appear to be straight even if you should wobble a bit as you sew. By following along the fold with the side of the presser foot, the quilting line will be straight without effort.

Sashing preparation: Please refer to the Layout/Cutting Guide in appendix to determine the length needed for your layout. Identical yardage is required for front and back sashing. (Each front sashing piece will have a corresponding back sashing piece and a piece of batting.) Tear front and back sashing strips 5" wide. Cut batting strips 4¼" (batting strips can be pieced if necessary).

Label cut sashing strips:
- Betweens — front
- Betweens — back
- Vertical strips — front
- Vertical strips — back
- Perimeter sashing — front
- Perimeter sashing — back

Optional:
- Borders — front
- Borders — back

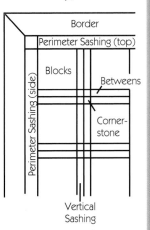

The finished width of the sashing will be 4". (An extra 1" is allowed for seam allowances and the mock string tuck.) Carefully iron front sashing strips in half, lengthwise, right sides together.

THE BETWEENS

The sandwich: Make a sashing sandwich from which to cut betweens.

- Backing, wrong side up.
- Batting, centered.
- Folded top sashing strip.

Align the sashing layers by placing a pin ¼" from fold of front sashing. Place a pin to mark center of batting. Align pins. The folded edge will extend ¼" beyond the center.

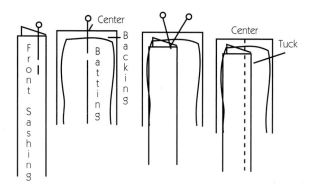

Sewing with the even feed foot:
Sew with ¼" seam allowance.
Sew entire strip length.

- Needle will stitch ¼" in from fold.
- Maintain a straight stitching line.

Be prepared and avoid problems. Calculate a shrinkage factor. Before sewing/quilting strip, mark off a 36" section on stripping.

HINT

The Shrinkage Factor

If an even feed foot is not being used to quilt sashing strips, there may be some shrinkage as the long strips are sewn. While this is not a problem with the betweens since they will be cut after being quilted, it could be a problem when using cornerstones in the vertical sashing.

After stitching sashing strip, measure the original section again. Calculate shrinkage per yard, if any. Divide by 3 and calculate shrinkage per 12". Use this factor if using cornerstones.

Pressing: Open up folded sashing strip and press gently. Turn strip over and press the back side.

Additional Quilting: If blocks have been heavily quilted, you may choose to add quilting rows 1" on either side of the first stitching line. Use quilting guide on even feed foot, if available or mark quilting lines by laying straight rows of ¾" masking tape along center stitching line. Guide edge of even feed foot next to tape and quilt ¼" away from tape using thread to match fabric.

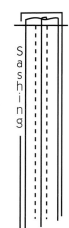

Cutting the Betweens: Use your personal number (block measurements). Cut 16 (20 for king) betweens. Be exact! All betweens must be the same size.

The sashing process may sound complicated, but after the first strip you will marvel at how easy it is and how fast it goes.

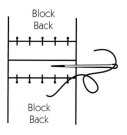

Join blocks with betweens creating a column.

With right sides together, join lower edge of block to between, sewing through:

- all layers of block
- front between sashing and batting
- do not catch in back of between.
- Trim any batting extending beyond stitching. Continue adding blocks in columns. Slightly larger blocks will be eased into between.

To finish back:

Fold under the seam allowances on back of between. Work on a flat surface. Place folded edge slightly over stitching line. Pin in place. Sew by hand with small, secure, blind hem stitch; or blind hem by machine! (This is like putting in a skirt hem.)

- •Regular presser foot
- •Set machine to blind hem stitch
- •Stitch length: 1½"
- •Stitch width: 1½"
- •Thread in needle and bobbin to match back fabric

Fold to sew:

- •Back of block is up
- •Between is under block

Sew with blind hem setting:

- •Straight stitches will fall on wrong side of turned-under seam allowance.
- •Zigzag stitch will catch edge of block but will not show on right side. A slight ridge will be created on back. It will press flat.

Back of Block

> ### HINT
> Please make a sample and give this timesaving method a try. Join all blocks into columns. Measure columns and record measurement on quilt diagram.

Lynn Karpay and her columns.

Gertrude Braun and her sampler.

THE EMERGING QUILT CORE

Vertical sashing will join the completed columns into the quilt core. The quilt will now begin to grow rapidly in size. Place a table next to the sewing chair to accommodate the bulk. A table on the far side of the sewing machine will catch the quilt as it is sewn, avoiding sudden lurches as the fabric shifts.

VERTICAL SASHING

The vertical sashing can be constructed like the betweens in one long row. For an additional color accent, add a cornerstone to the strip.

CORNERSTONES

Cornerstones are colorful squares inserted at the intersections of the horizontal and vertical sashings. Not only do they add a spot of color, but they also serve as a useful construction aid in helping to align the blocks horizontally. Cornerstones are pieced into the long sashing strip before the strip is layered and quilted.

Cornerstones can be added at each intersection of the quilt. A 20" block quilt would have 30 cornerstones. Another option is to use cornerstones only in the central portion of the quilt. In that case there would be 12 cornerstones appearing in the 20" block format.

MAKING THE CORNERSTONES

Buy ½ yard of fabric that enhances those in the quilt. Cut two or three 5" strips across the grain depending on need. Fold strips in half, right sides together. Sew entire strip length, ¼" from fold (No batting or backing used now). Open strip and press. Cut into 5" segments. Squares will now measure 5" wide, 4½" top to bottom.

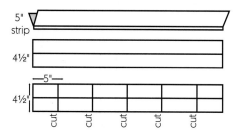

Add cornerstones to sashing. Cut the front sashing strip into segments, using your personal number plus allowance for shrinkage, if necessary. Join sashing to cornerstones. (Tuck will run from side to side.) Fold and iron strip in half lengthwise. Lay strip on backing, batting sandwich. Fold of sashing will extend ¼" beyond center. Stitch center line. Use even feed foot.

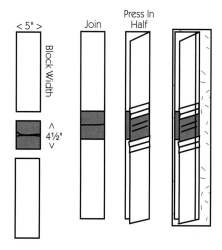

> ### HINT
> Additional rows of vertical quilting can be added to the sashing strip, but a second row of stitching cannot be added on either side of the horizontal tuck in the cornerstone at this time. After the quilt core is completed, additional rows of stitching can be added to the cornerstones, if desired.

JOINING BLOCK COLUMNS TOGETHER

Join columns one and two. Position vertical strip on inside edge of column one, right sides together. Carefully match cornerstone seam lines with horizontal seams. Repeat for columns three and four. Join sections together with last vertical strip. Trim out excess seam line batting. Finish back with blind hem stitch.

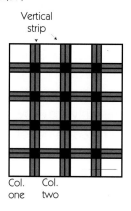

VERTICAL STRIPS WITHOUT CORNERSTONE

The decision to use cornerstones is strictly arbitrary. They do help align the blocks in straight horizontal rows. If they are not used, however, the same benefit can be achieved by carefully marking the vertical strip with temporary but precise lines where cornerstones would have been. Assemble vertical sashing strip. Quilt strip. Using personal number (sewn block), mark intersections on vertical strip. Measure width of between to calculate cornerstone depth. Compare all marked strips to make sure markings are identical and accurate.

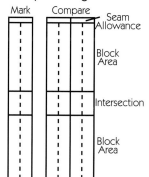

JOINING SASHING TO COLUMNS

Position sashing on block column. Align markings with betweens. Sew sashing to block column. Trim out any excess batting. Finish back with blind hem.

PERIMETER SASHING

If no borders are to be included on the quilt, the perimeter sashing will frame and finish the quilt. The outside edge can be beautifully finished into a knife edge before it is applied to the quilt. This eliminates the need for an additional binding.

CONSTRUCTION OF KNIFE EDGE FINISH

Press sashing strip in half lengthwise, right sides together. Open up pressed strip as only one raw edge will be sewn. Layer front and back sashing, right sides together. Place batting underneath. Sew outside edge with ¼" seam allowance. Do *not* trim batting from seam allowance.

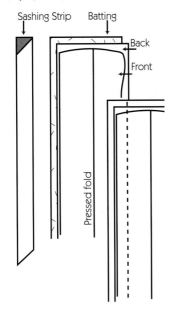

Turn sashing, right sides out, enclosing batting. Establish attractive outside edge by rolling seam line slightly to the back and pinning frequently to maintain edge. Fold strip into position and quilt the tuck ¼" from fold. Remove pins. Gently press sashing strip and outside edge.

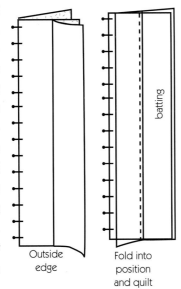

The finished outside strips are ready to be applied to the quilt core. Measure the quilt length again, this time through the center of the quilt. This is very important if you are to have quilt sides that hang smooth and straight. If the quilt sides are too long, the sides will ripple or wobble. If the sides are too short, the quilt will draw up and possibly buckle slightly. This is an important step in the final appearance of the finished quilt.

APPLYING QUILT SIDES TO QUILT CORE

Quarter the side sashing. This means locating and marking the midpoint, quarter, and three quarter divisions of the side. Find the corresponding reference points on the quilt core: ¼, ½, ¾. Match and pin reference points together. Stitch sashing to quilt. Turn and finish back of perimeter sashing.

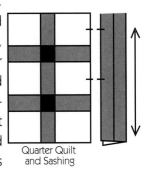

Quarter Quilt and Sashing

FINISHING TOP AND BOTTOM SASHING

The top and bottom perimeter sashing strips will be finished on the corner edges as well as the long sides. The sashing will be prepared and then applied to the quilt like adding a waistband to a skirt. The previous sashing had a folded tuck that had been stitched to form the quilting. These strips must also have the hidden tuck but the sewing will be a little different. The ends must have the tuck sewn first so the corners can be finished. Read and understand the directions before you begin. It isn't difficult, it's just different.

Measure the horizontal width of the quilt through the center of the quilt. Use this measurement to determine the final sashing width plus seam allowance. (If you used the shrinkage factor to determine vertical sashing length, use it here also.)

Cut sashing strips and batting the desired width.

Press front (top and bottom) sashing strips in half.

Sew tuck ¼" from fold in front sashing only.

Press sashing open. Layer batting, back, and sashing (tuck fold toward raw edge).
Sew outside edges:

- Do not stitch the bottom seam allowances.
- Keep edges to be sewn together. Lower back edge will extend ½" below front sashing.

To finish strip: Turn strip, right sides out. Pin to establish final edge. Fold sashing out-of-the-way to expose tuck. Sew tuck from end to end as far as possible, sew over the previous stitching line.

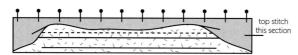

top stitch this section

Quarter quilt core and top sashing. Match reference points. Sew finished strip to quilt, right sides together. Finish back and celebrate!

BINDING – AN OPTIONAL QUILT EDGE FINISH

Traditionally, a ¼" finished binding has been used as a way to finish the edge of a quilt. When you choose to do this method, use fabric from your quilt which will either match or contrast with the outer edge. Do not use commercial binding since the fabric and color will not match those used in the quilt. The binding can be cut lengthwise or across the grain. It does not need to be cut on the bias unless it will be stitched around a curved edge.

BINDING WIDTH AND APPLICATION

A 2" cut strip generally produces a well-filled ¼" binding. However, before cutting the quilt binding it is a good idea to make a mini-quilt sample with fabric and batting. This will help you to determine the exact binding width for your quilt as well as give you practice with the technique. The binding strip will be folded and sewn double to the right side of the quilt. When it is pulled to the back, the folded edge should just cover the initial stitching line. Lightweight batting may require a thinner

binding strip of 1⅞"; heavier batting requires a little more than 2" wide strip. All joining seams in the strip should be on the bias.

MAKING A BINDING SAMPLE

Make a 9" square quilt sandwich with leftovers from your quilt and batting. Cut binding strips on the cross grain of the fabric.

- Cut strips 2" wide.
- Cut enough to create strip 48" long.
- Join strips with a bias seam.
- Lay ends perpendicular to each other, right sides together.
- Stitch across strips making a diagonal seam.
- Trim seam allowance to ¼".
- Press seam open.

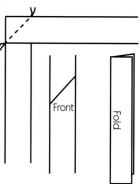

Front / Fold

Fold strip in half, wrong sides together. Align raw edges of quilt and binding. Start stitching binding near the center of one side, leaving a free tail of 8". Sew with ¼" seam allowance.

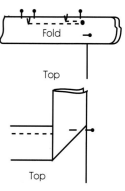

Raw edge of quilt / Tail

Stop sewing ¼" from end.

- Lock stitches.
- Cut threads.
- Remove quilt from machine.

Fold binding, forming a 45° angle.

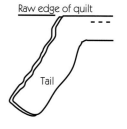

Fold / Top

- Finger press fold line.
- Pin in place.

Fold binding in downward position:

- Place fold even with side one raw edge.
- Raw edge of binding will be even with side two.

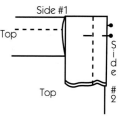

Side #1 / Top / Side #2 / Top

Sew from top of fold to next corner. Repeat for other sides.

Sew to within 6" of initially sewn binding, lock stitches, and remove from machine.

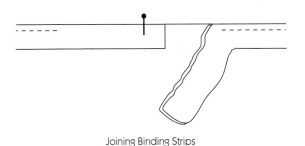

Joining Binding Strips

Mark center of unsewn portion of quilt with pin. On left strip of binding, align raw edges with quilt, cut 1" beyond the pin. On right strip, cut 1" to the left of the pin.

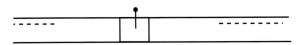

On right strip cut 1" to the left of the pin.

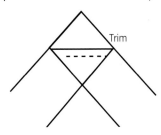

Open both strips and place ends right sides together. Join with bias seam. Trim excess from corner. Press seam open.

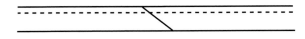

Refold strip and finish stitching it to the quilt.

Fold binding to back of quilt. Slipstitch in place with tight, invisible stitches. Stitch miters closed with matching thread.

To restate: Overlap the two ends of the binding by the width of the cut binding strip. In this case strips are cut 2"; overlap is 2". The binding will be applied to the quilt in the same manner.

WRAPPED BINDING

This binding variation is used mainly on wallhangings when you do not wish to interrupt the visual line of the quilt with another element. The binding is cut and initially applied in the traditional manner. This time, however, the binding is pulled completely to the back of the quilt and finished. It is a pleasing finish and almost unnoticeable even from the back when the binding fabric matches the back of the quilt. Cut binding strips 2" wide on cross grain of the fabric.

APPLICATION

Sides: Measure quilt from top to bottom. Cut two strips to this measurement. Fold strips and pin to front side edges of quilt matching reference points centers, and quarters. Before sewing, remove ¼" seam allowance from the ends of binding strip to minimize bulk in corners. Sew strip to quilt. Cut out any excess batting from seam line. Pull strip completely to the back. Blind hem by hand.

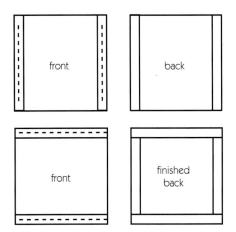

Top and bottom: Measure the width of the quilt. Add ½" to this measurement. Fold under the seam allowance on each end. Press strips in half lengthwise; folded seam allowances will be on the inside of strip. Apply strips and finish as above.

Note: Binding can be finished with machine blind hem if desired.

T ake pleasure from the last steps of finishing your quilt. Don't rush the process; enjoy using your skills to complete a quilt that will hang straight and true whether you choose to place it on a wall or put it immediately on your bed.

A FINISHED QUILT IS A JOY INDEED!

GOAL OF LESSON EIGHT
• To complete quilt

SKILLS
• Borders
• Miters
• Hanging sleeve

BORDERS

Borders are meant to complement a quilt while extending its size. Borders are a final frame for your blocks. Often the fabric chosen is deeper in value than the sashing. Border fabrics should be an extension of the quilt and relate to those used in the quilt. The border can be one fabric, or it can be pieced.

A border that is 10" wide or less works very well both aesthetically and mathematically. For the back of the border 3½ yards have been set aside. Now you must decide on the front border.

The outside edge of the border can be finished first, eliminating the use of an additional binding. The border will be assembled and quilted before being attached to the quilt core following the directions for perimeter sashing. Quilting must not extend into the ½" edge reserved for joining.

Large cornerstones or pieced blocks the width of the borders can be used to finish the outside corners of the quilt borders. They will be added to the top and bottom border strips before they are added to the quilt.

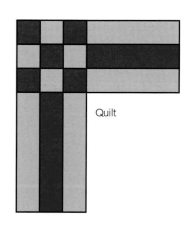

Quilt

Your batting may be in pieces. It is all right to piece the batting scraps together with a wide zigzag stitch. Keep the batting stretch going in the same direction if it has a definite grain line.

BORDER CHOICES

Repeat the sashing fabric in the border. If you choose to use your sashing fabric in the border, the perimeter sashing and the border can be treated as one wide strip. Quilt with free-motion stitching or a continuous line stencil pattern.

Strip piece two or three fabrics together. A strip pieced border is easy to make and coordinates well with the quilt if the fabrics or colors chosen also have appeared in the quilt. Either a Nine-Patch checkerboard square or a miter make a pleasing corner finish. For added texture and interest, one of the strips can be a gathered or rouched.

Summertime Sampler by author.
AQS Museum Collection

Instructions for gathered strip: Cut and piece a 2" strip of fabric three times the length required for plain strips. Machine wind elastic thread on the bobbin using a slow winding speed. Insert bobbin into bobbin case. No bobbin case adjustments are required.

Gathered Strip:
- Sew with slightly less than ¼" seam allowance.
- Set stitch length at 4, or long stitch.
- Sew the entire length of strip.
- Repeat for other edge of strip.
- Replace elastic thread with regular bobbin thread
- Sew gathered strip to first border strip. Pin strips right sides together, have gathered strip on top. Even out gathers as you sew, if necessary. Sew with ¼" seam allowance.
- Sew other side of gathered strip to next border strip, adjust gathers, pin joining strips.
- Sew with ¼" seam allowance.

Quilt by stitching in the seam line.

From Misty Morning by author.

Use a decorative stripe or a print fabric. Decorative stripes or prints add a great finish to the quilt, especially if some of the fabric has already been used in the quilt. A decorative stripe has design elements which repeat. The most pleasing effect is achieved when the borders are mitered and all four corners of the quilt appear to be identical in design. This will occur if the same design motif is placed at the midpoint of each border strip. This does not ensure that the design will be whole and complete, but the corners will at least be identical.

Directions for striped border placement: Cut borders using fabric design as your guide for the exact width. Lay borders on quilt with centers of one motif at midpoints of quilt sides. Fold corners into miter to appraise design created. Your stripe probably has several motifs. It also has a space between motifs.

Experiment with different design areas at the quilt

midpoints. If corner designs are still not right, take a few tiny tucks in corresponding border strips to shorten border and improve corner design. Quilt using free motion stitching around design motifs.

Cutting the borders: To make the back finishing easier, the back of the border fabric should end up being at least ¼" wider than the front of the border. Refer to your personal number record to determine border length. If you plan to miter the border, add two times the border width to the length of the border plus one design repeat. It is better to cut these too long than be ½" too short!

Example: Quilt core is 85" long. Borders are 10" wide times two. Design repeat is 4". Cut border 109".

Assembling the borders:
Layer backing and border fabric right sides together, batting on the bottom. Sew outside edge. Turn borders, right sides out. Do not trim batting from seam allowance. Establish crisp edge with pins. Quilt strip in quilt core area only. Do not quilt the mitered areas. Leave ½" seam allowance unquilted.

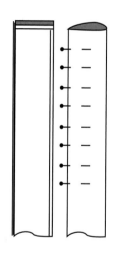

Apply Borders:
• Quarter quilt and borders.
• Position identical motifs on opposing midpoints.
• Match reference points.
• Sew borders to quilt.
• Start and stop seam ¼" from edge of quilt.

The miter: Start this job when you are rested. Work on a large, flat surface. Smooth side border up in continuous straight line. Smooth top border out in continuous straight line. Trim excess from top and side borders but leave ½" seam allowance.

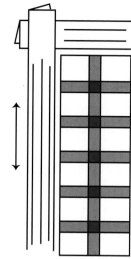

Fold seam allowance to the inside. Fit side border into top border ignoring extra batting momentarily.

Fold top border only into a 45° angle, matching design elements if applicable. Use matching thread to hand sew miter with small invisible stitches. Trim away excess fabric and batting on inside of mitered area. Baste

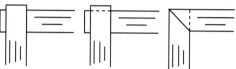

batting sections together. Finish back with miter or straight corner. Quilt corners.

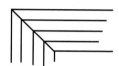

Golden Memories of Christmas by author.

DOCUMENTATION

Each quilt has its story to tell. The circumstances leading up to making the quilt as well as the episodes of life occurring during the quiltmaking process are all memorable. Record these along with the names of the blocks and any other pertinent information on a label and sew it to the back of the quilt. Include the name of your quilt, your name, address, date, and size of quilt. Why not include a picture of yourself, the quiltmaker, on the label? Attach the label to lower right hand corner of quilt back.

THE HANGING SLEEVE

If you ever contemplate hanging your quilt or entering it in a show, you will need a hanging sleeve attached to the top. Attach it now while the leftover quilt fabrics are at hand. A 4" finished sleeve will meet your needs.

Directions: Cut 10-13 9" squares of remaining scrap fabrics. (Scraps create an available supply of fabric if needed for quilt repair.) Join them togeth-er into one long strip the width of quilt plus 2" for finishing. Turn under short ends and stitch. Sew long sides, right sides together, to make a tube. Turn sleeve right sides out. Use blind hem to secure top and bottom edges of sleeve to quilt top. Option: Use a 9" strip of fabric for hanging sleeve rather than piecing.

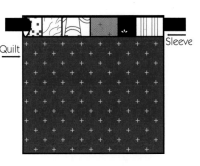

To hang quilt: Select a spot away from bright sunlight. Attach large wooden drapery rod brackets to wall. Hang quilt on heavy wooden rod. Make more quilts and change decor often.

QUILT CARE

You will certainly try to protect the finished quilt from fading and abusive wear and tear. Do not be an overly protective parent, however, who just hides the quilt. Use it but be aware of keeping it out of the way of strong sunlight and sharp objects. Air the quilt occasionally if possible or fluff in the dryer without static free dryer sheets if you feel it needs a little freshening.

The quilt may be washed occasionally in a home washing machine using the gentle cycle and a gentle detergent. Agitate briefly and then let the quilt soak for about five minutes. Repeat agitation/soak with the rinse cycle. Use warm or cold water. Remove immediately at the end of the final cycle to avoid the possibility of one fabric fading or running onto another. Dry in the dryer until slightly damp and then spread on the bed.

If the quilt has been made as a gift, include washing instructions. Suggest to the recipient that the quilt need not be washed often. You might even volunteer to wash the quilt for them.

A GALLERY OF SAMPLER QUILTS

Beginning on page 122 you will find directions and templates to make your own "Touches of Turquoise" sampler quilt.

DANCING UNDER THE RAINBOW

SPRING PEEPERS FOR MY BROTHER

CRABTREE CORNER

RANDOM WALKS THROUGH THE LATTICE PATCH

MISTY MORNING

ASIAN DELIGHTS

SANTA CLAUS IS COMING TO TOWN

GOLDEN MEMORIES OF CHRISTMAS

AFRICAN SERIES 1

AFRICAN SERIES 2

THE RIBBON DANCER

NEW DIRECTIONS

DANCE OF THE SPRITES

MORE THAN A CENTURY OF BITS AND PIECES

TOUCHES OF TURQUOISE

DANCING UNDER THE RAINBOW
78" by 94", 1995
by Beth Rice, Catonsville, Maryland

Taking Lois's Sampler Class with a friend was great fun. We pored over every quilt in her book. Once we had completed a few blocks, we had the confidence to expand our search for inspiration. Things I learned were to focus on learning; buy extra fabric for those inevitable mistakes; remember that any block can be replaced later; stay flexible. Making this quilt was more work than I expected. It was also more educational, more fun, and more rewarding than I had anticipated.

SPRING PEEPERS FOR MY BROTHER
62" by 92", 1996
by Kathy Goodwin, Rockville, Maryland

This is my first quilt. I began it four months after my brother Scott died in a mountain climbing accident in Colorado. He was 31 years old. Our love for each other inspired, anchored, and made us more hopeful human beings. I wanted his spirit to shine through in this quilt. The use of vibrant colors and spring peepers (frogs) added Scott's exuberance and mischievous sense of humor to the quilt.

CRABTREE CORNER
78" by 94", 1996
by Jean Crabtree, Rockville, Maryland

When this quilt was finished, I laid it out on my living room floor. As I stared at it, I felt a sense of awe to think that I had really made this beautiful quilt. In my world that is busy with three small daughters, it is wonderful to have my own creative outlet that brings me so much satisfaction and a sense of accomplishment. I really love my quilt and everything that went into it.

RANDOM WALKS THROUGH THE LATTICE PATCH
78" by 94", 1995
by Leslie S. Montroll, Gaithersburg, Maryland

This quilt won an award at the Montgomery County (MD) Fair. The title is a double play on words. The blocks represent random selections from the world of quilt patterns with lattice referring to the sashing. The quilt's title pays tribute to my late father-in-law, Dr. Elliott Montroll, a physicist who did extensive research and writing on the randomness of phenomena. The lattice refers to the crystalline structure of molecules.

MISTY MORNING
97" by 105", 1988
by Author

When the early morning haze floats over an English garden, all the world seems quiet and peaceful. A Liberty of London fabric was the key fabric for this quilt. Other fabrics I chose were slightly muted. Many added texture or embellishments before being sewn into blocks. Ultra-Suede® tulips decorate the sashing. The ruched sashing strip is flanked by a decorative border print.

ASIAN DELIGHTS
78" by 97", 1989
by Author
from the collection of Maureen Hendricks, Potomac, Maryland

Asian designs meld with traditional American patterns to produce a bicultural sampler quilt. The Ocean Waves block contains a stitched Japanese coda for ocean waves. The same blending of cultures is found in the Maple Leaf block. The kimono is a copy of a patchwork coat for a Japanese general made in the sixteenth century. The simple Nine Patch became an original Japanese Lantern block. The Oriental man and lady were taken from linen coasters from Japan.

Best of Show, Fredericksburg, VA, 1989.
Blue Ribbon, National Quilting Association Show, Takoma, WA, 1989.
Red Ribbon, AIQA, Houston, Texas, 1989.

SANTA CLAUS IS COMING TO TOWN
76" by 90", 1995
by Author

Traditional blocks take on an aura of the holidays in this red-and-green Christmas quilt. Appliquéd Santas embellished with metallic thread add an easy but festive touch. The Drunkard's Path is trimmed for the season with holly. Random lamé stars decorate the sashing. Favorite holiday recipes and pictures of my three granddaughters make this a special memory quilt.

GOLDEN MEMORIES OF CHRISTMAS
83" by 99", 1988
by Author

Traditional and original blocks capture the glow of the Christmas season in this holiday sampler quilt. Family pictures and carefully selected block patterns make this a treasury of meaningful family mementos. Made for my daughter, Kristen Curling.

Best of Show, AIQA, Houston TX, 1988.

AFRICAN SERIES 1
28" by 28", 1995
Carole Liebzeit, Cincinnati, Ohio

African fabrics totally transformed these traditional sampler blocks. The blocks are joined with a bold center striped sashing and then cut apart and reassembled.

The end result is a striking piece strong in rhythm and depth.

AFRICAN SERIES 2
45" by 45", 1995
Carol Liebzeit, Cincinnati, Ohio

Eight sampler blocks and African fabrics produced this unique wallhanging. Narrow, bright sashing fabrics separate the blocks. Four blocks set on point provide a medallion center framed and embellished with dancing buttons. Fabric inspired swirls spread over the surface adding motion and texture.

THE RIBBON DANCER
56" by 56", 1996
(named by Christa Smith)
Judy Lundberg, Silver Spring, Maryland

When a design catches your imagination, ideas whirl. Making a series of quilts is not only possible, but often necessary. "Ribbon Dancer" is the fourth in a series of off-center log cabin explorations. Each quilt took a step away from the traditional symmetry. The lucky use of the red fabric with purple and white splashes adds sparkle and pizazz. The quilt consists of two 2-color blocks and one solid color block. Turning the blocks this way and that, or setting them on point, opens wonderful possibilities.

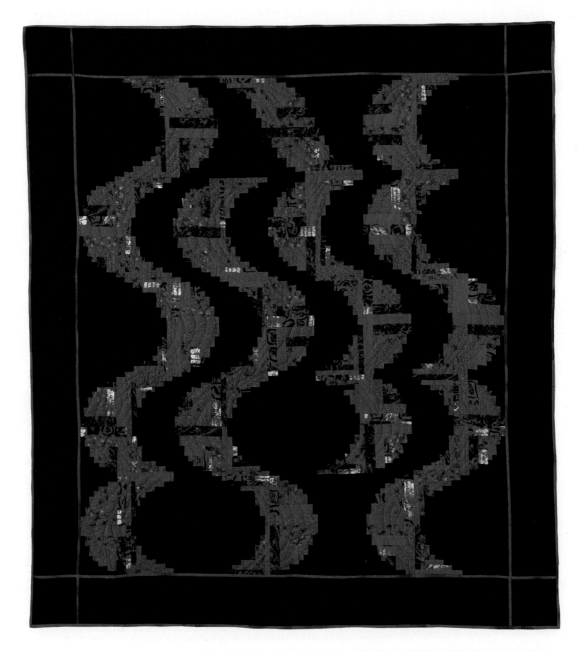

NEW DIRECTIONS
63" by 63", 1995
by Author

This is the fourth in a series of quilts influenced by Japanese art and design. The block is an adaptation of Wayward Wind by Kumiko Sudo. Machine sashiko stitching using two threads in one needle was used for quilting.

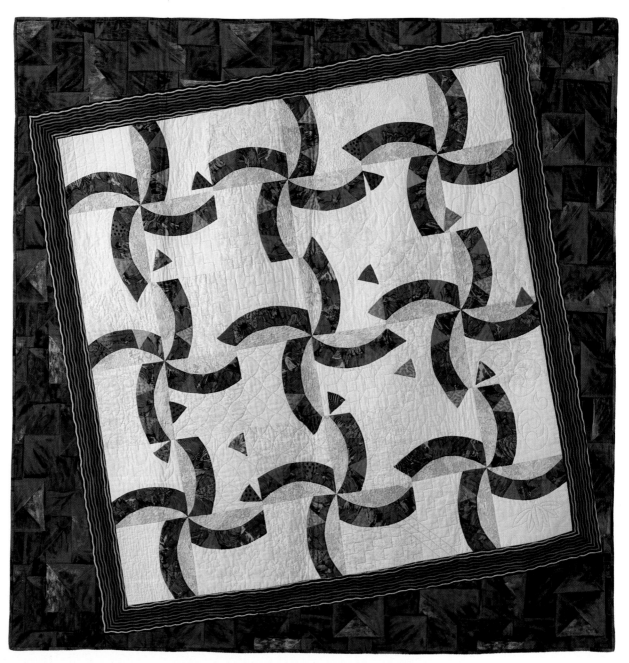

DANCE OF THE SPRITES
58" by 68", 1989
by Author

"Dance of the Sprites," based on the Pinwheel block, expresses feelings of mourning and hope while experiencing the illnesses of two friends. The lower left portion of the quilt in grays represents sadness and self-contemplation of mortality. The upper right quadrant represents heaven and transition. The pinwheels are the spirits or souls. They are left free and not quilted in the main body of the quilt to show strength and vigor. In the upper right corner they are still visible but blend into the background indicating integration and calm.

MORE THAN A CENTURY OF BITS AND PIECES
68" by 84", 1991
by Author

"More Than a Century of Bits and Pieces" is a time line linking the quiltmaker of the present to the quiltmakers of the 1880s. This is a scrap quilt using rescued blocks and vintage fabrics with some of today's reproduction prints. Some of the blocks were used in their original condition; others were recut and re-pieced using the original designs. The quilt was divided into four workable but uneven sections for quilting. The sections were later joined and borders added. Stenciling was used to indicate dates and inventions of the period.

TOUCHES OF TURQUOISE
68" by 84", 1991
by Author

"Touches of Turquoise" is a vibrant Medallion sampler featuring sharp, high contrasting color values. The central design is expanded by a series of borders surrounded by 14 theme-sharing blocks. The fabrics for this quilt were collected on a trip through the Southwest. While the fabrics themselves are not handwoven or indigenous to the area, the colors speak of a brilliant Southwest summer. Design sources include books on Indian art, baskets, and jewelry; a trip to the Indian exhibit at the Field Museum in Chicago; and a search of traditional quilt patterns with Indian-related titles.

AWARDS

• First Place, National Quilting Association Annual Show, 1990.

• Best in Show, Montgomery County, MD, County Fair, 1990.

• Second Place, Houston Quilt Festival, 1990.

• First Place, Sotterly Plantation Show, 1991.

• First Place Machine Quilt, People's Choice, Best Use of Color, Cook Forest Center for the Arts, 1991.

• Best of Show, People's Choice, Quilting in the Tetons, 1992.

DIRECTIONS

Make the fourteen 12" sampler blocks first to develop your own sense of theme and color contrast. Then make the center block.

BLOCK ONE — INDIAN TRAIL

Indian Trail

This is a Four-Patch design. Divide center square so block can be made with four 6" blocks. Small half square triangles can be speed pieced, if desired.

¼ of center square

BLOCK TWO — CEREMONIAL FACE

Permission granted from Kittie Spence.

Cut face adding seam allowance. Place ¼" folded strip on face markings:

• Fold edges of 1" strip to center to equal ½".

• Fold strip in half to equal ¼".

• Use blind hem stitch to appliqué.

Stitch or appliqué Ultra-Suede® facial features. Gather face edges and pull over template.

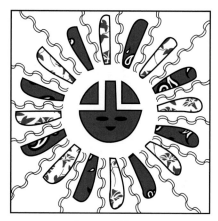

Ceremonial Face

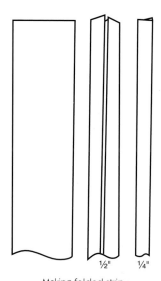

Making folded strip.

Appliqué face to background. Appliqué 16 sunrays using faced shapes or other appliqué methods. Align rays on backing. Quilt additional rays with 4mm double needle and wavy or serpentine stitch. Use metallic thread and decorative stitch for additional interest around face.

> **HINT**
> When more than four seams are being joined at an intersection, it is a good idea to pin the intersection first. Then machine baste the intersection (about 1") to check alignment.

BLOCK THREE — TRADITIONAL FISH BLOCK

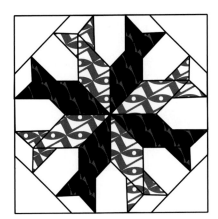

Fish Block

Be precise in cutting and piecing. Leave seam allowances free when piecing. Stitch fish together. Add 8 fin/background/fin units. Set in diamonds. Add corners. Quilt fish with scales.

set in diamonds

BLOCK FOUR — INDIAN STAR

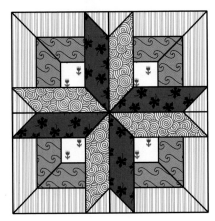

Indian Star

Piece in quarters. Add Indian decoration/beads. Quilt with decorative stitches.

BLOCK FIVE — TEEPEE VILLAGE

Teepee Village

Use ¼ square templates from:
- •Nine-Patch bottom row (#6)
- •Four-Patch second row (#4)
- •Five-Patch third row (#6)

Add 5½" by 12½" strip for sky.
Make some flaps that open:
- •Cut extra triangles.
- •Fold through center.
- •Seam bottom edge. Turn.
- •Include raw edges in block construction.

Quilt teepee poles and other details.

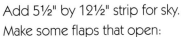
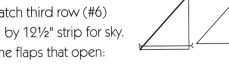

BLOCK SIX — THUNDER AND LIGHTNING

Thunder & Lightning

Finish and apply six thunderclouds. (Please refer to clamshells.) Use ¼" black bias tape for lightning. Add buttons on braided cord for rain. Appliqué strip over raw edges of thunderclouds and ends of rain cords. Outline quilt the design with free motion quilting.

BLOCK SEVEN — A GILA MONSTER NAMED JIMMY

Use faced shapes for body parts. Use Ultra-Suede® for legs. Embellish with assorted beads. Use triangles of any size for corners.

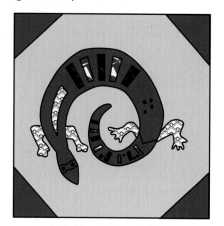

A Gila Monster Named Jimmy

BLOCK EIGHT — THE ANVIL

Please see Four-Patch designs. Embellish with beads on a string. Use blanket stitch to add stitching interest on center squares.

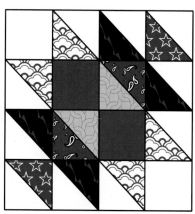

The Anvil

BLOCK NINE — SQUASH BLOSSOM

Create rumpled "quilt skin" (pg. 154) and then cut trapezoid. Embellish with conches and beads. Quilt with decorative stitches.

BLOCK TEN — ARROWHEAD

Try for a transparent effect in center. Fill light areas with decorative stitches.

BLOCK ELEVEN — ARROWHEADS

Large triangles are cut in two pieces to simplify piecing. Piece in strips.

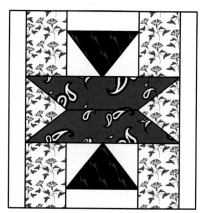

Squash Blossom

Arrowhead

Arrowheads

BLOCK TWELVE — KACHINA DANCER

Design idea from jewelry catalog. Use rumpled "quilt skin" for dancer. Use faced-shape appliqué. Silver metallic fabric is used as facing fabric. Edges show giving impression of silver and turquoise. Add silver stitching to dancer. Embellish with silver beads. Appliqué on simple strip pieced block.

Kachina Dancer

BLOCK THIRTEEN — TRIPLET

Pattern from Kansas City Star, 1933. Use Nine-Patch templates.

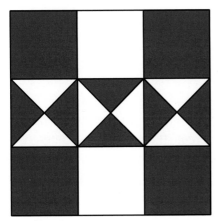

Triplet

BLOCK FOURTEEN — LIGHTNING BLOCK

Four-Patch templates. Simple block with bias or ¼" strip lightning appliqué.

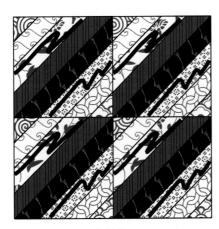

Lightning

THE CENTRAL MEDALLION

The medallion or central block is originally a 12" block which has been enlarged to a 24" block and then turned to sit on point. While it may look complicated, it is really a very simple block when approached as a square.

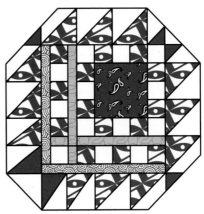

Hat Creek

Used with permission of Kittie Spence.

Hat Creek Medallion

FILLING IN THE BLANK SPACES

Borders surround the block and change it from a square to a rectangle large enough to fill the space. Large triangles and space strips of the background fabric will have to be added.

Using graph paper to diagram the layout of the 12" blocks and the 4" sashing, you can see that the central portion will be approximately 28" wide by 44" long.

Jumbo rickrack edges the top and bottom of the central block. The inner rectangle is framed by black cording. Curved strip piecing is used in the medallion and in the borders.

CONSTRUCTION

Construction techniques follow those used in the sampler quilt. Triangles were appliquéd to the mock string sashing for highlights.

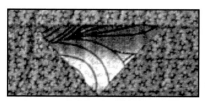

Sashing Appliqué

CURVED STRIP PIECING

Select two contrasting fabrics A and B. Cut strips 1½" larger than desired finished width. Layer A and B, right side up, one on top of the other. Use rotary cutter and wiggle through center area two times. You will have cut two borders — one to use now and one for a later project. Select either ABA or BAB combination. Lay border fabrics on flat surface. Mark reference points every 5". Place fabrics right sides together, matching reference points. Sew, easing edges together.

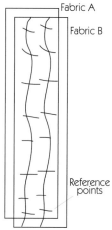

Fabric A
Fabric B
Reference points

> **HINT**
>
> Border corner design may not align for a flowing miter. This can be very effective. Squares can be appliquéd over corner joints if desired.

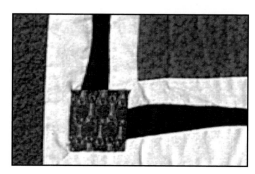

Corner Border Appliqué

THAT WAS FUN!

The completion of a quilt leaves you ready to make another. Great! There are many different types of quilts that you can make for family members and friends. The familiar blocks from the sampler quilt can become the basis of many beautiful and unique quilts.

Allow yourself time to explore new possibilities. Strive to make each quilt better than the last. Try at least one new trick in each quilt. Share your quilts and quilting ideas. Enter quilt shows. Acquire more quilting buddies. Attend a quilt conference annually. Nurture your passion!

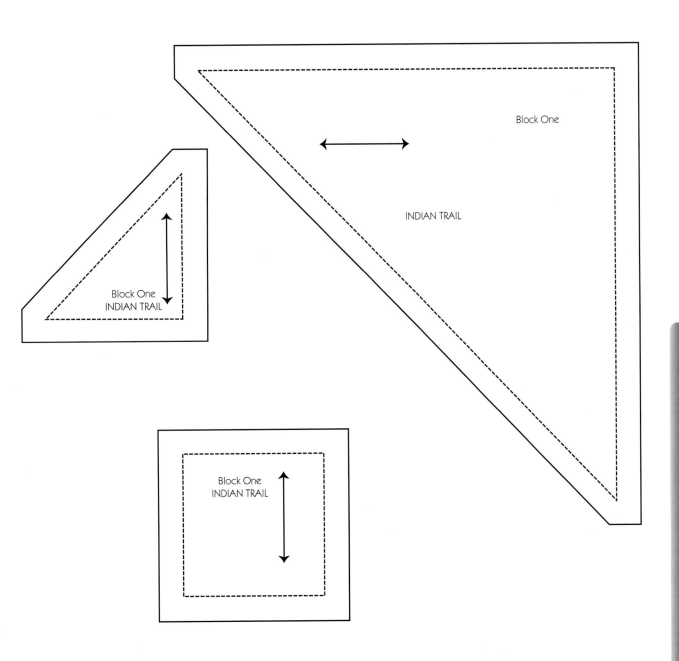

Block One

INDIAN TRAIL

Block One
INDIAN TRAIL

Block One
INDIAN TRAIL

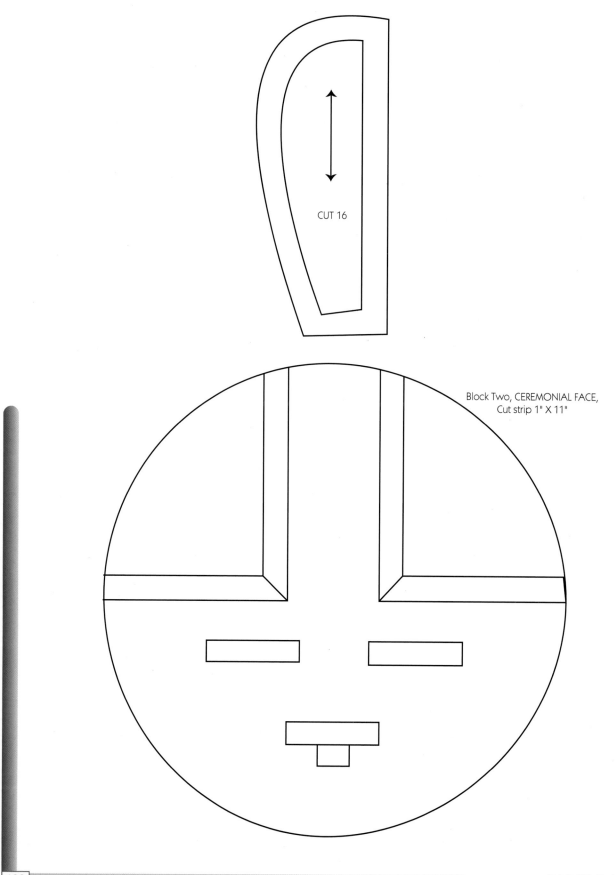

CUT 16

Block Two, CEREMONIAL FACE,
Cut strip 1" X 11"

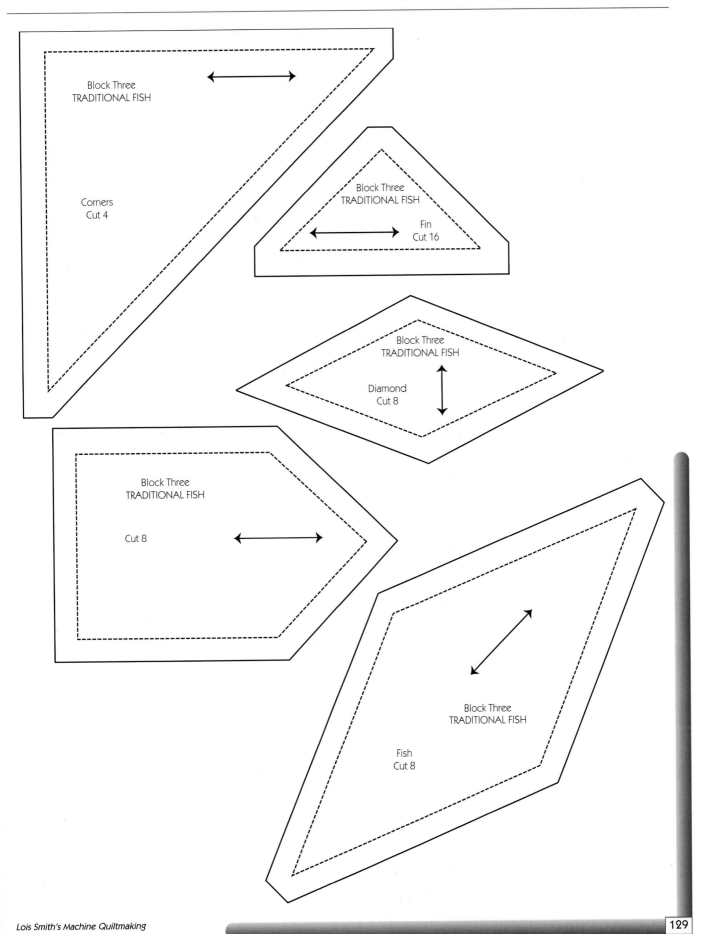

Block Three
TRADITIONAL FISH

Corners
Cut 4

Block Three
TRADITIONAL FISH

Fin
Cut 16

Block Three
TRADITIONAL FISH

Diamond
Cut 8

Block Three
TRADITIONAL FISH

Cut 8

Block Three
TRADITIONAL FISH

Fish
Cut 8

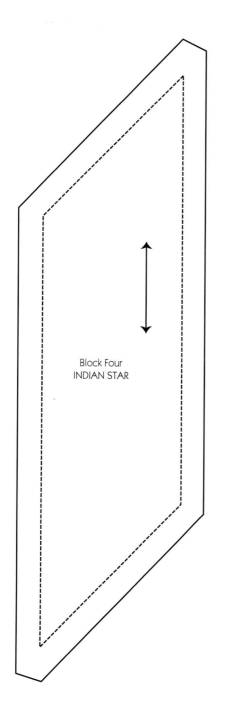

Block Four
INDIAN STAR

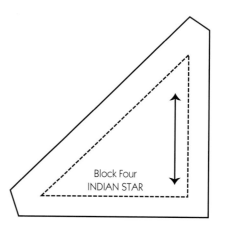

Block Four
INDIAN STAR

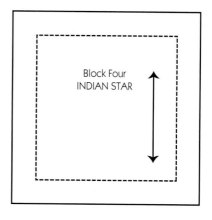

Block Four
INDIAN STAR

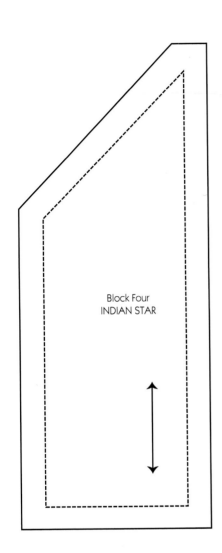

Block Four
INDIAN STAR

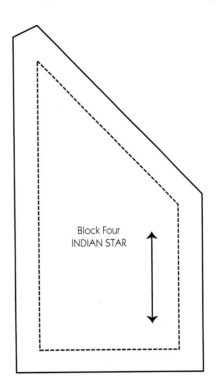

Block Four
INDIAN STAR

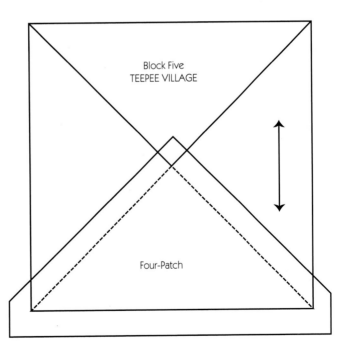

Block Five
TEEPEE VILLAGE

Four-Patch

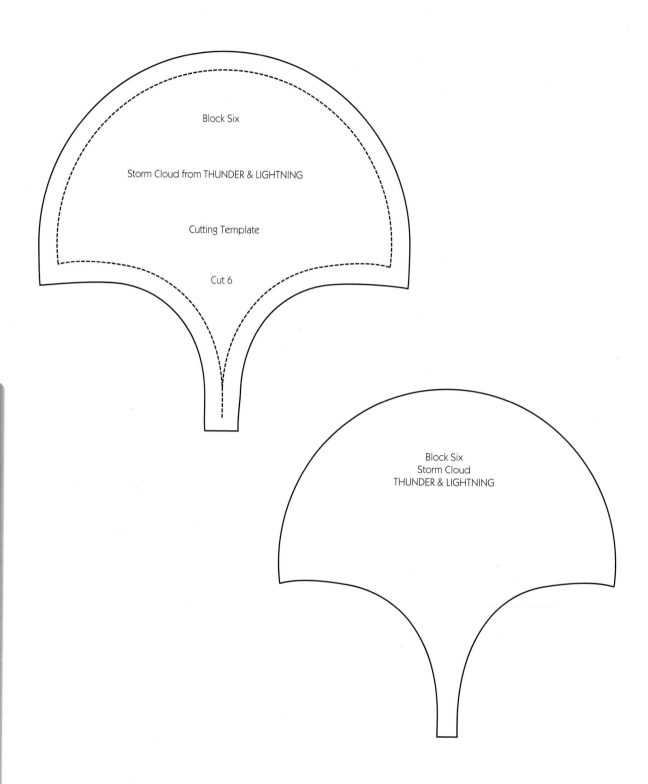

Block Six

Storm Cloud from THUNDER & LIGHTNING

Cutting Template

Cut 6

Block Six
Storm Cloud
THUNDER & LIGHTNING

Appliqué
Template

Appliqué Template

Appliqué
Template

Block Seven
A GILA MONSTER NAMED JIMMY

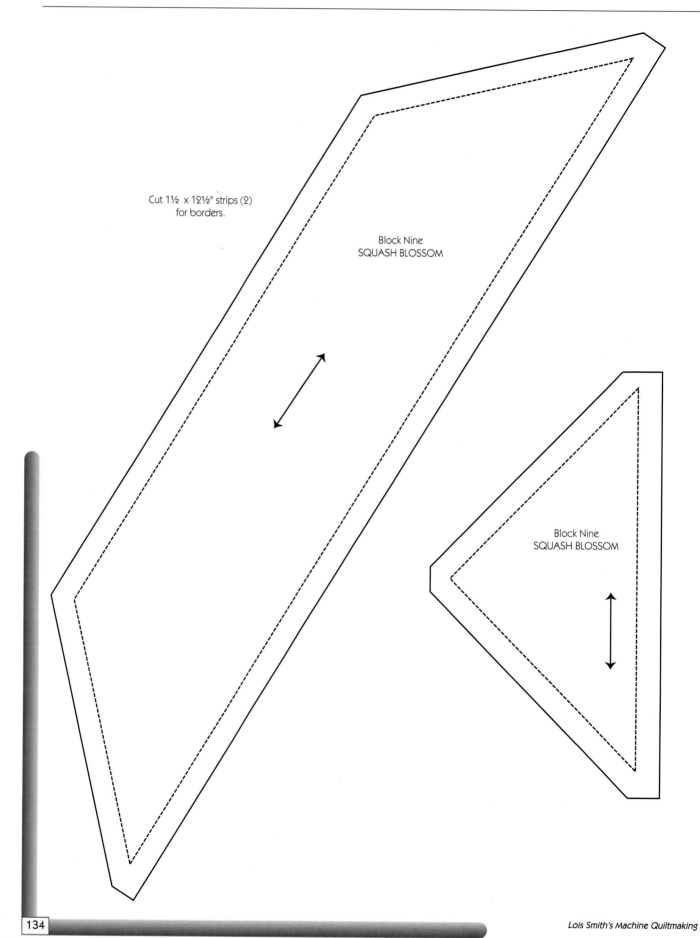

Cut 1½ x 12½" strips (2)
for borders.

Block Nine
SQUASH BLOSSOM

Block Nine
SQUASH BLOSSOM

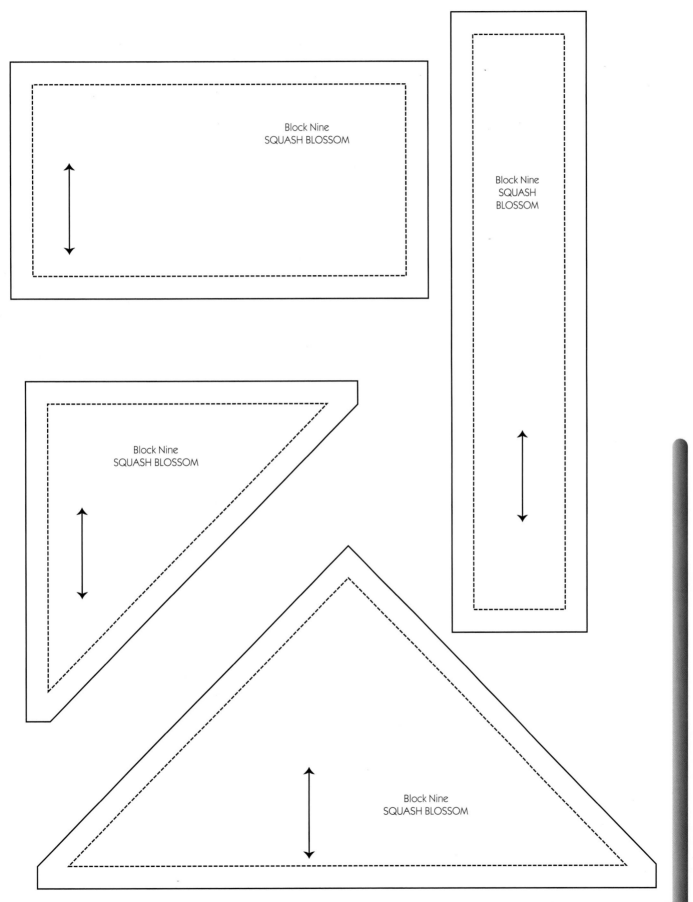

Block Nine
SQUASH BLOSSOM

Block Nine
SQUASH BLOSSOM

Block Nine
SQUASH BLOSSOM

Block Nine
SQUASH BLOSSOM

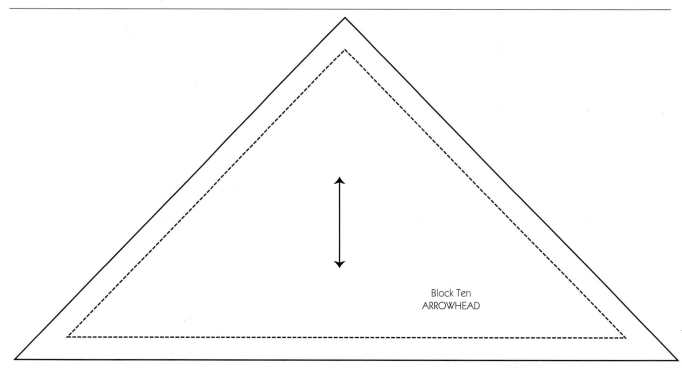

Block Ten
ARROWHEAD

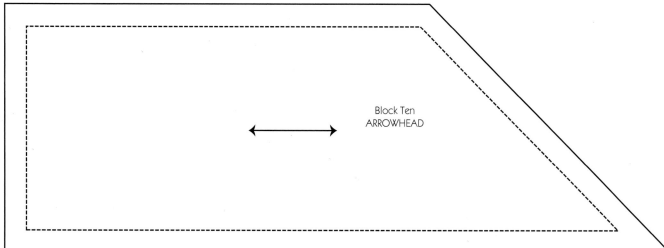

Block Ten
ARROWHEAD

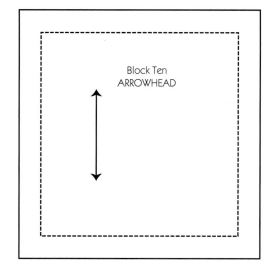

Block Ten
ARROWHEAD

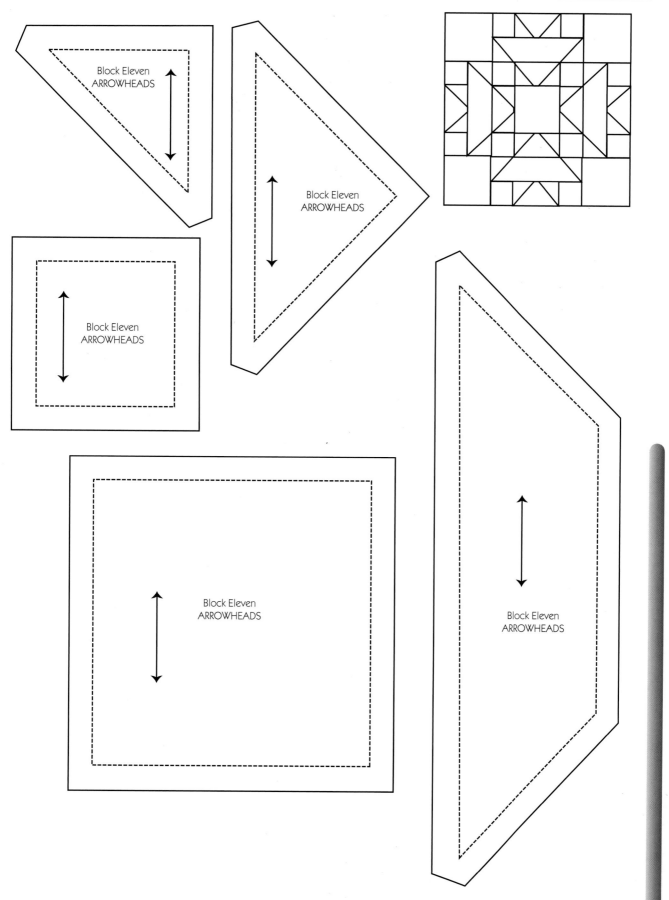

Block Eleven
ARROWHEADS

Block Eleven
ARROWHEADS

Block Eleven
ARROWHEADS

Block Eleven
ARROWHEADS

Block Eleven
ARROWHEADS

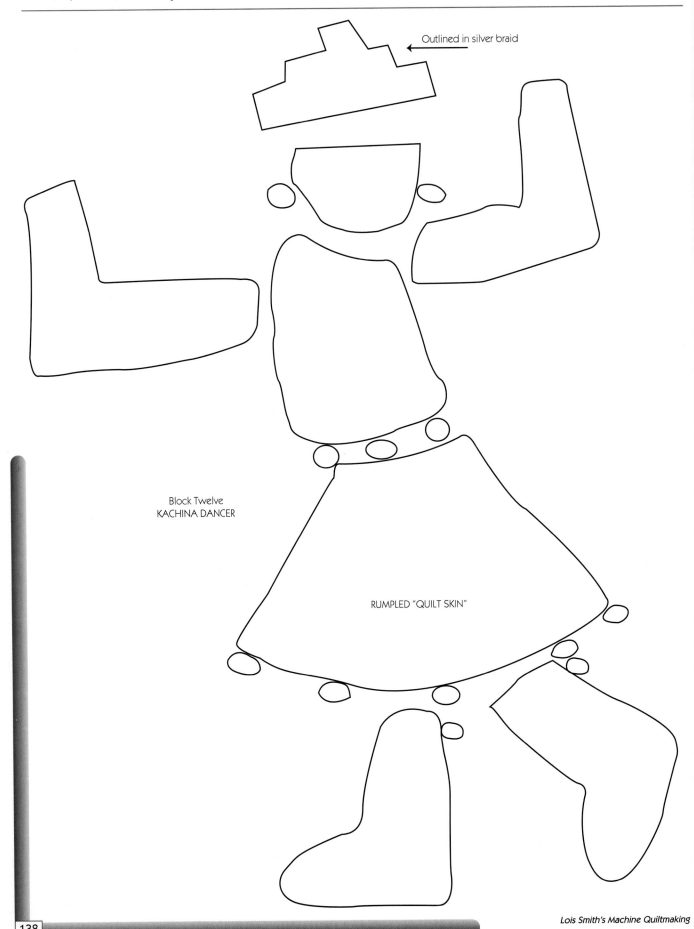

Outlined in silver braid

Block Twelve
KACHINA DANCER

RUMPLED "QUILT SKIN"

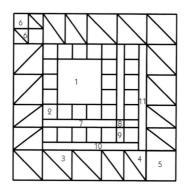

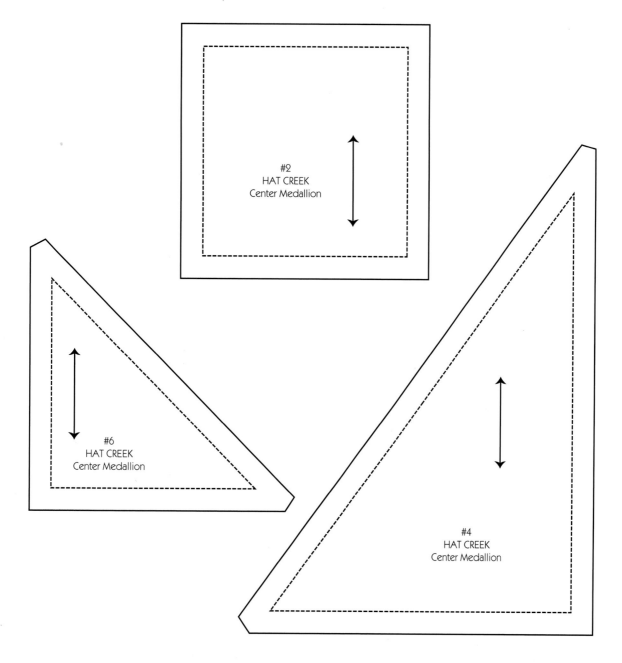

#2
HAT CREEK
Center Medallion

#6
HAT CREEK
Center Medallion

#4
HAT CREEK
Center Medallion

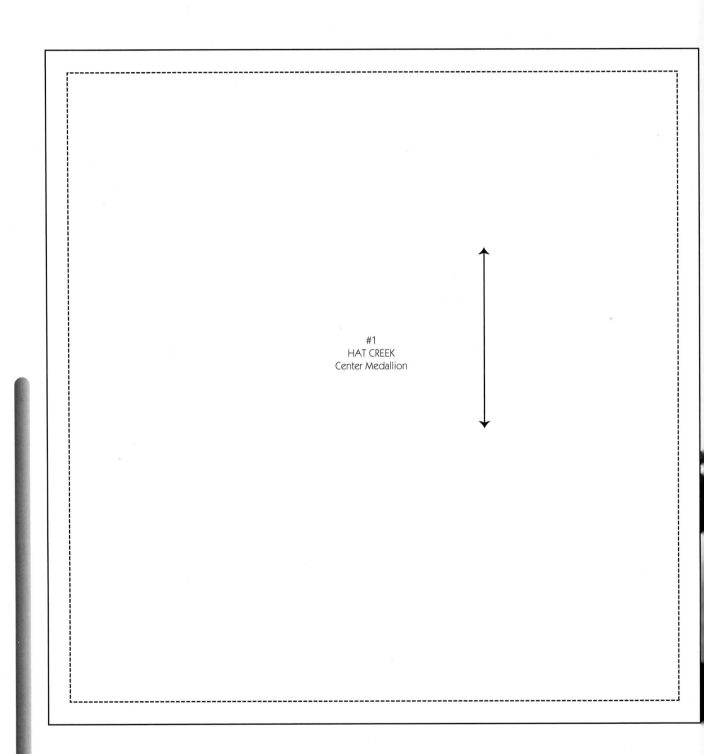

#1
HAT CREEK
Center Medallion

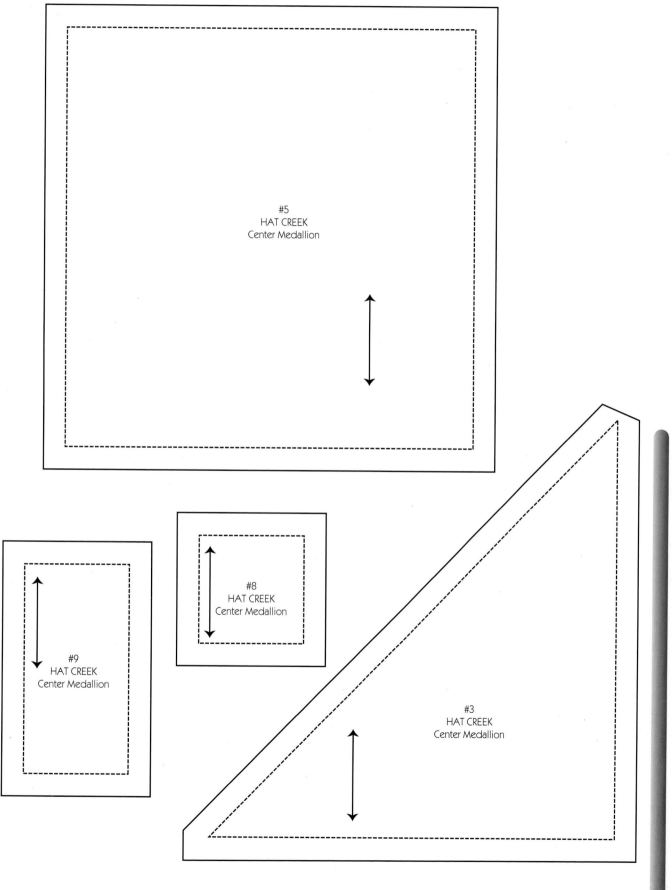

#5
HAT CREEK
Center Medallion

#8
HAT CREEK
Center Medallion

#9
HAT CREEK
Center Medallion

#3
HAT CREEK
Center Medallion

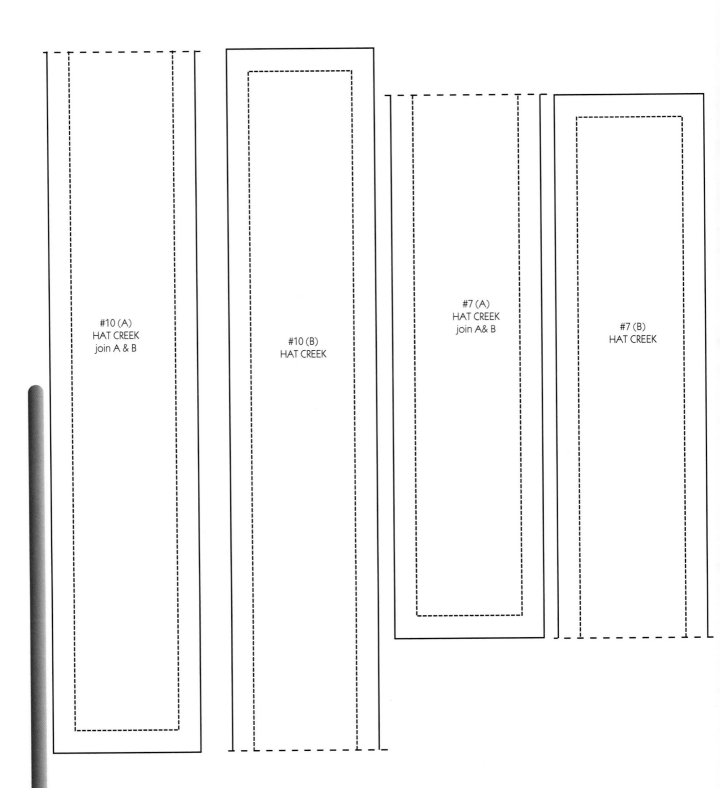

#10 (A)
HAT CREEK
join A & B

#10 (B)
HAT CREEK

#7 (A)
HAT CREEK
join A& B

#7 (B)
HAT CREEK

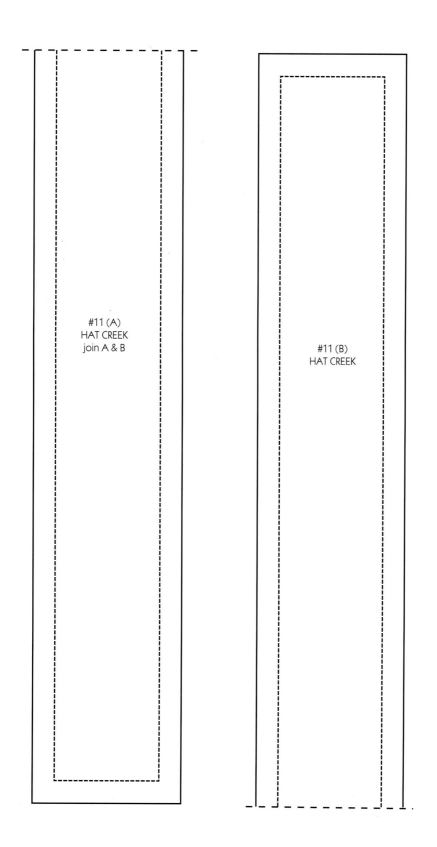

#11 (A)
HAT CREEK
join A & B

#11 (B)
HAT CREEK

Playful Additions

My soul, will wither and blow away if I fail to play with color and to experiment with silly and ridiculous things on a daily basis.

COLOR — THE RAINBOW — THE SUNRISE — THE SUNSET

Color is so fundamental and yet so illusive. Without even an awareness of it, we are influenced and directed. You might say our lives are molded by the colors that envelop us. Our spirits soar on a sunny day and slump during the gray of winter.

Color is a most potent element in quilts as well. It is what makes you stop to admire one quilt over another in a show. When organizing fabrics and colors for the sampler quilt, it was suggested that an outstanding fabric be selected and colors pulled from it to develop a working palette. This is one approach. Another approach is to work with the color wheel which adds a cognitive element to the emotional appeal. Color choices are then generated from a broader internal base.

Everyone wants to make that outstanding quilt, but not every quiltmaker feels comfortable putting the colors together. Some have stumbled onto a favorite color scheme and are afraid to break out to try new combinations. The reality is that behind each color-confident quiltmaker has gone many hours of study, deliberation, and perhaps liberation. Smashing color schemes are not an accident.

What then can be done to develop the color confidence? The more you know and understand about the relationship of colors, the more perceptive you will be to their dynamics.

Color is not something that is learned exclusively by reading a chapter in a book or by memorizing the color wheel. Color is a lifetime revelation based on observation and trial and error.

There are some fundamental suggestions or color theories based on the color spectrum and its division and organization. These can help to give some concrete structure for developing combinations that might be new and exciting in your next quilt.

THE COLOR WHEEL

The color wheel visually illustrates the systematic relationship among colors. It is divided into the cool and warm colors. The cool hues are the evening shades of blue, green, and purple, which are very soothing. The bright, splashy colors are the warm colors which reflect all the energy of the sun and the earth. These are boisterous colors.

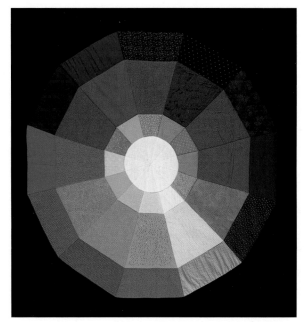

The Color Wheel

Cool colors are those between yellow-green and purple. Warm colors are those between yellow and red-purple.

VOCABULARY

Hue: the actual color. The attributes of a particular color that distinguish it from another color.

Value: the lightness and brightness or darkness of a color. Tints have white added to the color making them light and ethereal. Black creates shades which give depth and punch to a design.
  • "Dance of the Sprites," p. 119. All the values in this quilt are relatively light. The slight variation in the light values creates the design.

Intensity: the amount of gray in a color. High intensity colors are bright and clear. Lower intensity colors are soft and muted. Tones are the lower, dusty hues.

- •"Dancing Under the Rainbow," p. 107 Black sets off this sparkling example of high intensity colors. This is a happy, high energy quilt.
- •"Misty Morning," p. 111. This quilt has the feel of an English garden in the rain. All the fabrics used are an example of low intensity.

Contrast: the change in value that gives zest to a piece. High contrast is often dramatic, exciting, and high energy. Low contrast is tranquil and calm.

- •"Dance of the Sprites," p. 119. The ethereal feeling in this quilt is derived from the use of pastel fabrics and low contrast elements in both the central design and the borders.
- •"New Directions," p. 118. This features a design which contrasts strongly with the background fabrics.

Neutrals: Black, white, tan, and gray. Neutrals are generally "soft spoken" and are used to give life to the fabrics around them. Neutrals can dilute a color scheme that becomes too strong.

- •"Forest Floor" uses a large textured background in neutral colors to set off the greens of the fauna.

Color Harmonies

Color, like music, has harmonious chords based on sequence and balance. These color chords act as guidelines for artists and quilters alike. By studying the sets of hues that are known to be visually pleasing, you may be able to add something to your quilts that will take them from the ordinary to the extraordinary. Using a color harmony is an excellent steersman for the quiltmaker in choosing fabrics. If you desire to add a bit of another color not specified in the scheme, go ahead. There are no color police. A working knowledge of the color chords enables the quiltmaker to select fabrics with more ease and to stretch the limits of color harmony with creativeness and imagination.

Monochromatic Color Scheme

A monochromatic scheme uses only one color in a range of values and intensities coupled with black, white, and other neutrals. Diversity in textural fabrics will add interest to this restful combination. "Forest Floor" is an example of a monochromatic color scheme. It uses 14 different values, shades, and intensities of green fabrics combined with neutrals.

Forest Floor by author

Analogous Harmonies

Analogous harmonies consist of hues that are touching on the color wheel, presenting a blending or closely related scheme. These combinations are generally restful and depend on variation in value and intensity for interest. Misty Morning uses the cool combination of blue-violet, blue, blue-green, and green to convey the feeling of an early morning mist. Only a few touches of hot pink from across the color wheel break through the morning fog. In choosing fabrics for this piece, I tried to imagine seeing the fabrics in a mist. The various colors are unified by the amount of gray in each piece.

Misty Morning by author

COMPLEMENTARY COLORS

A complementary color scheme is based on colors that are opposite each other on the color wheel. This can be an exciting and vibrant. To extend your knowledge of complementary colors, take watercolor paints and mix two complements together in varying amounts. For example, mix a little green with a larger amount of red. Add more green and then more green. Equal amounts of red and green will yield a neutral.

Golden Memories of Christmas, by author
Best of Show, Houston Quilt Festival, 1989.

Complementary color dyes create a wonderful sweep of color. Notice the beautiful hues produced when the complements of yellow and purple are mixed together.

Complimentary Color Dyes

TRIAD (EQUILATERAL)

Triadic schemes are made from any three colors that are equidistant on the color wheel. Pick one color, skip three, and so on. As with any color harmony, the neutrals can be used to extend the color range. Frequent use of the neutrals dilutes the color scheme.

One color is generally dominant in the scheme. One of the three may be used only in small amounts as a zinger. It is, nevertheless, still important to complete and give balance to the color harmony.

TRIAD (ISOSCELES)

The isosceles triad starts with a pair of complementary colors across from each other on the color wheel. Use one of those selected but substitute colors on either side of the other complement. For example, blue-green and red-orange are the selected pair of complements. Instead of using the blue-green, blue and green complete the harmony.

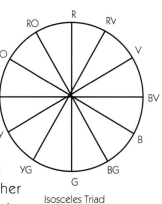

Isosceles Triad

"Tranquility" by author

This is a wonderful color scheme especially for nature scenes. Blue can be used for the water or sky, green for the grass and flower stems, red-orange for flowers or sunsets.

TETRAD (SQUARE)

The tetrad (square) harmony uses four equidistant colors. Pick one, skip two, and so on. Try to imagine a quilt using one of these color schemes.

Red orange — Violet — Blue green — Yellow
Red — Blue violet — Green — Yellow orange
Red violet — Blue — Yellow green — Orange

Next time you are snowed in or snowed under, take some time off and dig into your fabrics. Stack fabrics in one of the above color harmonies and see how it looks. Remember that although you are using four color families, one will still play the dominant role and one will be the zinger.

TETRAD (RECTANGULAR)

The rectangular tetrad uses two sets of complementary colors. To get started, select one pair of complementary colors. Do not use them, but use the two colors on either side. Teton Majesty is based on this color chord.

Teton Majesty by author

Yellow Orange & Yellow Green plus Blue Violet and Red Violet. The original, unused complement, was Yellow and Purple (Violet.)

HEXAD

The hexad uses six different colors. Pick one, skip one, and so on. When using such a range of colors, it is advisable to limit the range of values.

Dance of The Sprites by author

Blue green — Yellow green — Yellow orange — Red orange — Red violet

> ### HINT
> Quiltmakers often confuse the terms "fabrics" and "colors."
> • A monochromatic color scheme may have 23 fabrics but only one color. All the chosen fabrics are shades or tints of the chosen color plus the neutrals used.
> • A triadic harmony could have 50 different fabrics but only three different colors.
> •Neutral colors (black, white, tan, gray) can be used to dilute and unify a harmony.
> •White adds sparkle and highlights to a quilt. Just a touch of a bright color will add life and interest.

Fabric dyeing is an excellent way to know and understand more about colors and how they relate to each other. It is also a way to stash many great values of your favorite colors. The blending of complementary colors always produces a wonderful surprise of neutrals that can be the quiet force in a piece. Fabric dyeing adds an appreciation of color, value, and intensity to quiltmaking.

Thanks to the creativity and experimentation of quilters like Nancy Crow, Ann Johnston, Adriene Buffington, and others, the process of dyeing gloriously colored fabrics has been made so simple that it can be accomplished with little mess or physical labor. Hauling buckets and toting water is no longer a prerequisite to a collection of dramatic or carefully blended fabrics. Fabrics can be dyed in jars or in heavy duty gallon freezer bags, eliminating most of the physical labor.

DYEING TO KNOW MORE ABOUT COLOR

Hand dyed fabrics are recognized by their slightly irregular surface patterning which can look almost organic or floral in design. This effect can be achieved by crowding or scrunching fabric into a small container; this limits the flow of dye through the cloth which causes mottling. Fabric is created with unique color irregularities.

Hand-dyed Fabrics

FABRIC DYEING

DYEING IN A JAR
OR FREEZER BAG

•

VALUE
GRADATIONS

•

CREATING A SIX
OR EIGHT VALUE
DE-SATURATION

•

CROSS DYEING
COMPLEMENTARY
COLORS

•

BLENDING TWO
PRIMARY COLORS

•

OTHER
STRATEGIES
FOR DYED
FABRICS

FABRICS

Finish free fabrics prepared for dyeing (PFD) — will accept the dye, producing the most intense colors. These fabrics may be ordered through mail by the yard or in 20 or 50 yard bolts or rolls. The roll does not have a crease down the center and is generally preferred. (Please see Sources of Supplies.)

Perma-press or other finishes on the fabric will interfere somewhat with the bonding/dyeing process. These fabrics can be scoured or scrubbed by washing several times with detergent or synthrapol. This helps to remove the manufacturer's finish. Muslin and unbleached muslin are fairly inexpensive and dye well. The bleached fabrics dye with a crisp brightness. Unbleached muslin is slightly muted. The stronger the dye, the less apparent the difference in the base fabric.

DYEING: THE SOCIAL ELEMENT

Fabric dyeing can also add a social element to quiltmaking. It is something that can be done easily with two or more people creating a day of fun and productivity. Group dyeing also creates a backup fund of fabric in case of emergency. If your record keeping includes the fabrics that you dyed along with you partner, you can easily chase down a bit of fabric you might need in a pinch. Why not call your quilting buddy and try it?

DYEING IN A JAR OR FREEZER BAG

HINT
I have dyed my own fabrics and taught fabric dyeing for many years. This new method of dyeing in a jar is much simpler than the earlier days of bucket brigades and exact timing. And the results are great!

When dyeing from ½ yard up to 2 yards, jars or freezer bags work as containers to create brilliant colors in a small amount of water. Freezer bags take up less room and are lighter in weight than the jars. They have a tendency to leak at times and are slightly harder to manage without spilling. The jars are rigid and make filling and adding dye easier. They look beautiful sitting in bright sunlight.

The directions given are for dyeing ½ yard pieces of bleached or unbleached muslin in one quart jars or one gallon freezer bags. Larger pieces of fabric can be dyed by doubling the container size and other measurements.

Helpful Facts to Remember:
1 cup = 16 Tbs. 1 Tbs. = 3 tsp. 3 yds. = 1 lb. fabric

Fabrics:
• 100% cotton muslin, bleached or unbleached

Supplies:
• Procion® MX dyes
• Plain salt to open fibers
• Soda ash or washing soda (carbonate of soda) to set dye
• Synthrapol or detergent for washing fabrics before and after dyeing

Equipment:
• 12 or more wide mouth quart jars with lids or heavy duty plastic freezer bags. (Canning jars have measurements on the side and are easy to store in original box.)
• Measuring spoons
• Measuring cups
• Dust mask
• Rubber gloves

Safety Basics:
• Dye is toxic in powdered state. Do not inhale.
• Dyeing utensils should not be used for cooking.
• Wear a mask when mixing dye in powdered form.
• Wear gloves when mixing and measuring.

Procedure:
• Wash fabric and tear into ½ yd. pieces.
• Fill jars with chemical water (water, salt, and soda ash).
• Add dye concentrate. (See suggestions.)

- Add fabric.
- Place lid securely on jar.
- Shake jar vigorously.
- Place jars in sun or warm spot.
- Turn jars frequently during the first two hours.
- Turn occasionally for the next day or two or three.
- Rinse fabrics.
- Wash by color families in washer.
- Iron and store grouping together.
- Be sure to use them.

CHEMICAL WATER

A chemical water solution will be prepared that can be used with any of the following dyeing methods. It will contain a mixture of water, salt, and soda ash; it can be stored indefinitely.

Chemical Water: 1 gallon warm water,
½ cup salt, 4 tsp. soda ash

DYES

Procion® dyes are fiber reactive dyes which are sun and fade resistant. They come in a wide range of colors. In the powdered form they have a long shelf life, but must be used within three days when mixed with water. Values are determined mainly by the amount of dye used.

Dyes may aggravate existing respiratory conditions. Care should be taken to wear a mask when measuring powdered dye.

The amount of dye suggested in the chart below is for an entire dyeing sequence, not individual jars.

DYE REQUIREMENTS

Requirements based on dyeing eight ½ yd. pieces in eight jars.

DYE	
Pale	¾ tsp.
Medium	1½ tsp.
Dark	1 Tbs.
Really Strong	2 Tbs.

These dye proportions are starting points. It takes less red than indicated as red dye is very intense. On the contrary, it takes more yellow and also black as these dyes are not as powerful. Turquoise is a little slower to react than the reds and oranges. Fabric dyeing takes experimentation and willingness to accept surprises along with the known rewards.

VALUE GRADATIONS

Value gradation dyeing creates fabrics in a gradual sweep of values from dark to light. This wonderful array of values can add depth and highlights when used in a project. Any number of gradations can easily be achieved, but six to eight is generally sufficient. The process is a dye de-saturation.

A value de-saturation series originates with any dye or mixed combination of dyes. This dye is then divided systematically into six or eight containers, cutting the amount of dye by one half in each jar. Fabrics in a sweep of values are produced.

De-saturating of Yellow Orange
Formula: ½ Tbs. Yellow 108 and ½ Tbs.
Orange 202

I find the chemist's de-saturating by water/dye replacement method the easiest, safest, and most foolproof method to follow. It is easiest and safest because it involves only one measurement of the dye powder. It is foolproof because the process of adding a half cup of dye concentrate to each jar just becomes routine without having to consider many different measurements and amounts of dye.

CREATING A SIX OR EIGHT VALUE DE-SATURATION

The amount of dye (see chart) is mixed in a measuring cup with a small amount of water until a paste is formed. More water is added gradually to the mixture to make one cup of concentrated dye solution.

Half of this concentrate (½ cup) will be poured into container #1. More water is added to the concentrate to again make one cup. Pour ½ cup of dye concentrate into #2. Replace with water. This procedure continues until all containers have dye. There will be a half a cup of weak dye left in the measuring cup. This can either be thrown out or added to a mystery pot.

Procedure:
- Fill 6 or 8 jars with 2 cups of chemical water each.
- Make 1 C. of concentrated dye solution.
- Pour half cup of dye concentrate into first jar.
- Refill dye concentrate with plain water to equal one cup.
- Continue adding ½ cup dye concentrate to each jar and replacing with ½ C. plain water.
- There will always be ½ cup of dye left at the end.
- Add damp fabric to each jar.

De-saturating of Yellow Green
Formula: 1 Tbs. Yellow #108 and
1 Tbs. Green 711

CROSS DYEING COMPLEMENTARY COLORS

It is fun mixing complementary colors together. Red/Green, Orange/Blue, and Yellow/Purple are some suggestions.

For best results, work with at least eight jars. Start with one color at one end, the complement at the other. Keep the complements pure at each end. Cross dye the other jars. The middle area will produce unique neutral colors.

Procedure:
- Choose any pair of complementary colors. (I chose blue and orange.)
- Fill 8 jars with 2 cups of chemical water.
- Slightly separate the first and last jar.
- Mix one dye concentrate using formula for dark.
- Using de-saturating method, add dye to jars 1 – 7.
- Add fabrics and stir or shake.
- In an hour mix second dye concentration.
- Start at jar #8 and add second dye concentrate to 7, 6, 5, 4, 3, 2, excluding #1.
- Follow previous procedures.

Fabrics sunning on Chincoteague Island

Formula:
1 Tbs. #410 Turquoise
1 Tbs. #202 Orange

BLENDING TWO PRIMARY COLORS

Any two colors can be blended using the cross dyeing technique.

In this case, two primary colors will be mixed: blue and yellow.

Since only six jars will be used this time, every jar will contain some of each dye family. The pure colors of yellow and blue were not dyed by themselves.

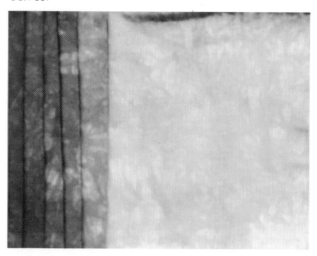

Blending Two Primaries:
1 Tbs. Yellow 108
1 Tbs. Indigo 422N

OTHER DYEING STRATEGIES

Using the complementary de-saturating technique, mix touching color on the 12-color Color Wheel. Example: blue and green; red and purple.

To deepen a hue, add a very small amount of black.

Adding the complement to a dye dulls the mixture.

HINT
Tuck a 1" x 4" swatch of like fabric in each jar as you dye. Record dye formula on swatch for future reference.

Formulas and dyes used in projects:
- Complementary Colors: Blue/Orange
    1 Tbs. #410 Turquoise
    1 Tbs. #202 Orange

- Blending Complementary Colors: Yellow/Purple
    2 Tbs. Yellow 108 (Yellow is weaker dye.)
    1 Tbs. Purple 804
    Jar #1 is only yellow; Jar #8 is only purple, pictured on p. 147
- Blending Two Primaries: Blue/Yellow
    1 Tbs. Indigo 422N
    1 Tbs. Yellow 108
    No parent fabrics dyes, only blended colors
- Light to Dark Sequence Yellow Green
    1 Tbs. Yellow 108 and 1 Tbs. Green 711
- Light to Dark Sequence Yellow Orange
    ½ Tbs. Yellow 108 and ½ Tbs. Orange

Please see List of suppliers for additional information.

Color is the essence of quiltmaking. Pastel fabrics can create a beautiful, restful quilt that is easy to look at and enjoy. Bright colors demand attention and are exciting. Warm color in quilts, red, orange, and yellow, give a bold, hot, and moving dynamic, while their counterparts of blue, green, and purple exude a feeling of coolness and calm. Fall imagery comes to mind when we admire the rust and gold fabrics.

Experiment with creating various textures. The perfect spot for application will present itself — and you will be ready!

If you visualize quilts hanging in a show, there are two levels of appeal: the impact of seeing the quilt at a distance and the close-up surprises that become apparent as you step nearer for a second glance. It is this second level of appeal that adds whimsy and deeper insight into the meaning of the quilt. Fabrics can be manipulated in a great variety of ways and still remain supple enough to be used in even the most traditional settings.

RUMPLED QUILT SKIN

Rumpled "quilt skin" adds interest to this Pinwheel and Squares block from the "Misty Morning" quilt. The fabric is first textured and then cut into the desired shapes.

Directions:
If you have the time, dampen yardage and scrunch into a small ball and tie with string. When dry, the fabric will be sharply creased and rumpled.

When in haste, dampen fabric and squeeze into a cup. Place in the microwave for two minutes and rotate. Process for two more minutes. (Don't try this method with metallic fabrics.)

Pinwheel and Squares block

In either case,the rumples can be fused to a lightweight interfacing or can be stitched to a lightweight fabric to preserve their rough integrity.

To Stitch Rumpled "Quilt Skin":
•Set up for free motion stitching.
•Stitch in the valley; preserve the ridges.
•Extra embellishments can be stitched under the folds for added interest.
Please note that in the previous section, p. 146, the entire background of "Forest Floor" was rumpled "quilt skin" with small "twigs" stitched under a few of the raised wrinkles.

Strips cut from this textured fabric can be used effectively in all forms of string quilting and log cabin. Rumpled "quilt skin" cornerstones add interest to the "Golden Memories of Christmas" quilt, p. 114.

ELASTIC THREAD

If I were stranded on a desert island, there are three things I would like to have with me: a sewing machine, fabric, and a spool of elastic thread! There is so much that can be done with elastic thread that I think you could spend days and keep on discovering exciting new textures.

Elastic thread is wound on the bobbin. It can be wound by machine using a slow speed. No additional change of setting is required when placing the bobbin in the case. If you have a spare bobbin case for use with decorative threads, you may choose to use it. Keep bobbin tension normal.

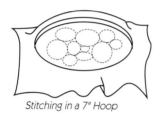

Stitching in a 7" Hoop

BUSHES, POPCORN, FLOWERS

- Set machine for free motion stitching.
- Elastic thread in bobbin.
- Normal or slightly tightened top tension.
- Fabric in 7" hoop.
- Make circles the size of a dime.
- Remove the fabric from hoop.
  The fabric will be gathered and
  have interesting tension pulls
  on the back.
- Steam the piece and watch the gathers
  draw even more.

This gathered piece of fabric can be cut without fear of loosing the gathers!

Dresden Plate with elastic scrunched center

"Fantasy Trip to Japan"
36" by 50", 1989, by Author

The three dimensional flowers in the foreground were made in a hoop with elastic thread in the bobbin. Instead of stitching circles the size of a dime, the rough outline of the flowers was stitched.

At the base of the tea house, pieced fabrics are gathered into a ruched strip giving the texture of rocks.

The stream is an example of rumpled "quilt skin." All of the trees and bushes are faced shapes.

RUCHED STRIPS

Ruched strips can be made by stitching on either side of a fabric strip using the regular presser foot and the feed dogs up. Three or more rows of parallel stitching will give the look of smocking with the advantage that it won't fall apart when cut.

Random stitching crisscrossing a piece of fabric will gather into incredible textures that could imitate rocks, a mass of flowers, or a boiling cauldron. All the elastic texture techniques above could be produced with or without batting under the fabric. The heavier the batting, the more controlled the gathers. Without batting, the elastic thread will draw the fabric even tighter.

SPECIALTY FABRICS

Dressmaker fabrics will often add a touch of reality or whimsy to a project. Collect them when they speak to you, and have them on hand for the day that you will need. This collection may include Ultra-Suede® scraps, lamés nettings, and metallic fabrics.

Last week the angle of the sun on the salt marsh outside my window made the water appear to be a bed of animated silver ribbons. The next day I walked through the fabric store and a bolt of silver mesh greeted me. I now have the components to complete a piece I have in mind.

DOUBLE NEEDLES

The 4mm double needle is a great needle to have in your collection. It stitches two threads at the same time which is economy of motion, if nothing else.

The wide spacing between the needles allows a ridge to form when a cording or grooved foot is used. The single bobbin thread forms a zigzag on the back pulling the fabric slightly. This creates the ridge on the front. When a flat-bottomed foot or a darning foot is used, two parallel lines result.

Bias tape: ¼" can be sewn with the 4mm double needle. Consider doing Celtic appliqué in which ¼" bias forms twisting patterns. In one pass the bias can be stitched on both sides.

The 4mm double needle can be used to quilt the borders with messages. Poetry or information about the quilt can actually be permanently included in the quilt by stitching calligraphy-like phrases in the border. First write your messages with a marking pen on a strip of paper equal to the border space available. Know what you want to say.

Then begin quilting through all layers with the darning foot. I often have to make a few word adjustments at the end. When quilting my Monet quilt,I had to add "grand and glorious profusion" in describing how the gardens grew as I had quilting space left.

DECORATIVE THREADS

Can you imagine an entire store with nothing but thread — some of it on cards, some on spools, others in small skeins? There are threads that are stubby, some that shimmer, and some that sparkle. There are threads in glorious colors; some even glow in the dark. Yes, all of these threads are available and waiting for you and your imagination to use them.

"A Return to the Garden"
44" by 44", 1993, By Author

These threads will be eye-catching in the quilt. You can use them to lead the eye around to observe various details. Decorative threads can help tell the story of your quilt. They are fun to use and are excitingly different. Use these threads with straight stitching, free motion stitching, or decorative stitches.

There are three ways to apply these threads to your quilt: by running them through the needle of your machine, by placing them in the bobbin and stitching from the backside of the quilt, and by laying them on the surface of the quilt and securing them with stitching — couching.

THREADS THROUGH THE NEEDLE

Decorative threads that are readily available include rayon, acrylic, metallic, and blended synthetic threads. In most machines these decorative threads work well and as easily as your basic threads. Select a decorative thread and give it a try. If you encounter problems such as frayed or broken thread, then consider using one of the needles designed especially for designer threads.

The needle: Start with the smallest size needle, 75/11, purposely designed to prevent shredding and breakage. For rayon and acrylic threads, a quilting needle or an embroidery needle is recommended. For metallics, the Metafil or Metallica needle is available with its slightly blunted point. If shredding or breakage still occurs, check to make sure that the thread is flowing freely and not hung up at the base of the thread pin. A thread stand helps to keep thread flowing.

- Schmetz Quilting Needle — sharp point, deep grove, enlarged eye
- Schmetz Embroidery Needle — blunted point, deep grove, enlarged eye
- Schmetz Top Stitching Needle — enlarged eye, deep grove, larger sizes
- Schmetz Metallica — 80/12 polished, elongated eye
- Beka Metalfil Needles — 80/12 deep grove, enlarged eye, treated with teflon

A silicone lubricant is available to help decorative threads flow through the tension disks and needle without fraying. It is generally applied directly to the thread by placing a line of lubricant the length of the spool. This really helps to keep thread flowing. If you have a computerized machine you may want to check with your dealer to see what your manufacturer suggests. A small piece of felt can be glued to your machine front and the silicone lubricant placed on it to lubricate the thread before it enters the needle but after the thread has passed through the tension disks.

The bobbin thread: A bobbin thread that is similar in weight to the needle thread is desirable. Fine nylon and polyester bobbin threads are available to pair with rayon and metallic threads, but these specific bobbin threads are only available in white and black. Fine basic polyester thread, not a heavy, multipurpose thread, that blends with the back of your quilt, will undoubtedly work well.

Thread weights: Threads come in various weights. Some threads are marked with the weight. A 30 weight thread is quite heavy; a 50 weight is fine; a 100 is very fine. Just by focusing on the feel of a thread, you will be able to judge whether it is fine or heavy. Experiement with both weights to determine your preference.

Bobbin adjustment: None generally required.

Top thread tension: Loosen slightly. This will help to balance the bobbin thread which will probably be a little heavier in weight.

DECORATIVE THREADS

Rayon thread comes in almost every color you can imagine. Its satiny luster is perfect for background quilting. It makes a piece virtually come alive. Two threads can even be run through the eye of a single top needle at one time to give added texture, whether you are using free motion, straight stitching, or decorative stitches.

Rayon threads come in two weights: the lighter is a 40 weight and glides easily through the needle; the heavier is a 30 weight and is more visible.

Variegated multicolored threads are available and excellent for meander stitching on a background composed of many different fabrics. The changing colors of the thread blend beautifully with the fabrics, eliminating frequent thread changes while creating a beautiful look on the quilt surface. Acrylic threads also come in a similar, glowing array of colors. I find them identical in appearance and use.

"Colorwash" by Author
(Metallic and Variegated threads)

Metallic threads are fun to use because they will sparkle and add an unexpected highlight to the quilt surface. The most reflective type is a thin, flat, ribbon-like, polyester film that is metalized with aluminum to make it brilliantly reflective. It is a knockout when stitched on black fabric! When using heavier metallics, use a larger size needle and loosen the top tension.

Cordonnet is a heavy, polyester buttonhole twist that can be used in the needle to outline a design or quilt sashiko patterns. It has a matte finish and-

---

HINT

On one occasion I stumbled onto a spool of metallic thread that refused to work well, no matter what I tried. I had used this exact type of thread successfully another time. I still had another spool on hand exactly like the offending thread. I tried it, and it worked perfectly. There are thread gremlins that like to tease. Keep a sense of humor.

---

comes in a limited number of basic colors; but it is great if you want some simple outlines for emphasis. A large needle and needle eye is a must with this thread.

THREADS IN THE BOBBIN

Some threads are too heavy to pass through the tension discs and/or a large needle successfully. These threads can be used in the bobbin. The sewing and quilting

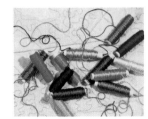

Bobbin Threads

can be done from the reverse side of the quilt. The beautiful threads will show on the top of the quilt. The top needle thread will show on the back of the quilt.

Machine tension: Again we will be stitching with threads that are unequal in weight. The bobbin thread is heavier than the needle thread. This time the tension on the top thread will have to be increased slightly to achieve stitches that are smooth.

Bobbin case: When working with the decorative threads, the bobbin may have to be loosened to allow the threads to pass freely through the bobbin tension. It is advisable to purchase a separate bobbin case to keep for such maneuvers. Mark the bobbin case in some way that distinguishes it from your regular bobbin case.

Needle: Almost any needle will work well. Try an 80/12 universal if you are in doubt. Stitch Length: Sew with a 3 or 4 stitch length which is close to a basting stitch length. These long stitches in heavy threads will show well.

Sewing speed: Sew slowly at a uniform speed.

Note: Leave thread tails at both ends of your stitching so they can be secured in the batting with a needle and thread.

BOBBIN THREADS

Ribbon floss: a silky, rayon ribbon that stands in relief on your fabric. It comes in many great colors. An off-white ribbon floss on off-white fabric creates wonderful, elegant designs.

Metallic Ribbon Floss: a glittery ribbon similar to above.

Pearl cotton: sizes 5 and 8. Comes in a little ball, but winds easily onto the bobbin.

Pearl crown rayon: A continuous rayon filament that comes in great lustrous and solid colors as well as many variegated colors.

SPECIAL EFFECTS

Use matching top thread to achieve the look of a solid stitching line. Use a top thread to match the fabric for stitching that looks like little beads.

Thinking backwards: It may take a little adjustment in thinking to stitch with the decorative thread in the bobbin. Designs can be transferred to the back of the quilt in the same manner as you would for quilting from the front. If you want to have your bobbin thread appear in a seam line or at a specific spot on a design, begin by stitching in the seam line with regular bobbin thread and invisible thread on top. Turn the work over, change the thread setup, and repeat stitching on the bobbin line, which is now visible. Remember, this is playtime, and you are having fun. Changing thread is not that difficult!

THREADS FOR COUCHING

Rich textured yarns and cords can be stitched to the quilt surface with dramatic results. This process of stitching threads to the quilt surface is called couching. Invisible thread can anchor the cord or a metallic thread could be used to add sparkle to the couched cord.

Suggested couching threads:
- Ribbons
- Yarn
- Bouclé
- Chenille
- Cords
- Twine

Machine setup:
- A cording or piping foot will help keep the thread in position when sewing straight or gently curving lines.
- Use invisible nylon thread for invisible couching. Use metallic or other decorative thread for special effects.
- Use a zigzag stitch:

  Set stitch width to cover couched thread.

  For yarns and bulky cords, use a small zigzag stitch and only nip one side of yarn. Push yarn over stitching line. No stitching is visible...magic!

THREAD DETAILING

French Knots by machine are so versatile. Depending upon how they are trimmed, they can appear as flower stamens, cat whiskers, or even as pampas grass along the shore.

Directions: Use a zigzag presser foot. Drop the feed dogs. Take two stitches in place. Make 6 medium size zigzag stitches. Return to straight stitch. Make two more stitches to secure thread. Repeat this process without cutting the connecting thread. When you have finished, cut the threads completely off or leave them to achieve the desired effect — fireworks, explosions, blossoms, etc.

Directions: Wind six or more strands of a decorative thread around a fork or piece of cardboard. Slip the threads off fork and twist into a figure eight. Secure the center twist onto the quilt with a tight zigzag stitch. Repeat this process until the detail is desired fullness. Cut the loops and fluff the threads.

HINT
In "A Return to the Garden" the thread twists were stitched over stamens from the silk flower department of a craft shop.

CUTTING LAYOUTS

Yardages are given for four different sizes of quilts. This should be an ample estimate of the yardage required for a SAMPLER quilt. The sashing requires identical yardages for the front and back of the quilt. Use the same cutting diagram for either yardage. The layout is planned so that none of the long sashing strips will have to be pieced. If you do not mind an extra seam in sashing, a smaller amount of fabric may be purchased.

If the sashing fabric that you have selected has a one way design, you may choose to cut the betweens and the top and bottom strips across the grain. Adequate yardage has been allowed but you will need to rediagram the front cutting layout.

FABRIC REQUIREMENTS FOR SAMPLER QUILTS
Based on 12" blocks
4" sashing

Bed Size	Crib	Twin	Double/Queen	King
Mattress Size	23" x 46"	39" x 75"	54" 75" 60" x 80"	76" x 80"
Finished Quilt	33" x 48"	68" x 84"	88" x 104"	104" x 104"
# Blocks	6	20	20	25
Sashing	3"	4"	4"	4"
Add. Borders	None	None	10"	10"

FABRIC REQUIRED FOR QUILT FRONT

Bed Size	Crib	Twin	Double/Queen	King
Blocks pcd.	2 yds. assrt.	7½ yds. assrt.	7½ yds. assrt.	8½ yds. assrt.
Borders	None	None	3½ yds.	3½ yds.
Sashing	No additional	4¼ yds.	4¼ yds.	5 yds.

Please note: To find the fabric that best complements blocks, purchase front sashing fabric after blocks have been completed.

FABRIC REQUIRED FOR QUILT BACK

Bed Size	Crib	Twin	Double/Queen	King
Backing Totals	3¼ yds.	7½ yds.	11 yds.	12 yds.
Blocks	3¼ yds.	3¼ yds.	3¼ yds.	3½ yds.
Sashing	for both	4¼ yds.	4¼ yds.	5 yds.
Borders	None	None	3½ yds.	3½ yds.
Batting	Crib size	90" x 108"	90" x 108"	King size

CRIB SIZE

Mattress . . . . .23" x 46"
Finished Quilt . . . . .33" x 48"
Blocks 6
2 yards assorted fabrics
Sashing size . . . . .3"
Back Totals . . . . .3¼ yds.
Includes front sashing
Batting . . . . .Crib size

Crib Back & Front Sashing

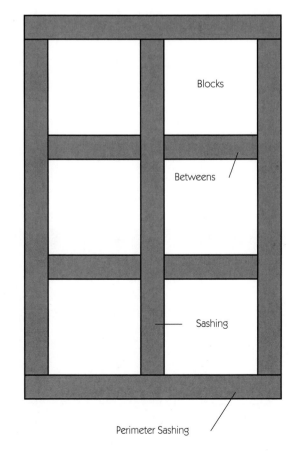

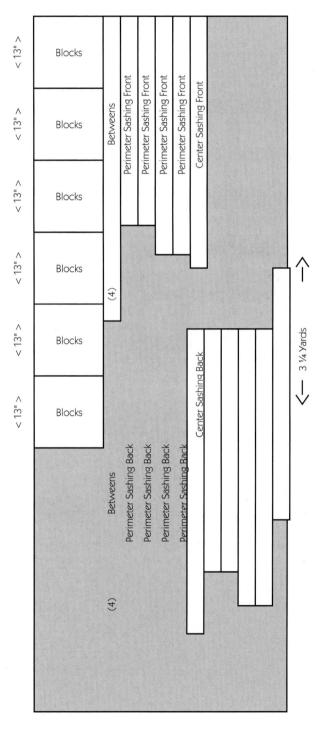

CUTTING LAYOUT

TWIN SIZE

Mattress . . . . .39" x 75"
Finished Quilt . . . . .68" x 84"
Blocks 20
Sashing Size . . . . .4"
Batting . . . . .90" x 108"

FABRICS REQUIRED

Blocks (front) . . . . .7½ yds.
Sashing (front) . . . . .4¼ yds.
Back Totals . . . . .7½ yds.
  Blocks . . . . .3¼ yds.
  Sashing . . . . .4¼ yds.

Back of Blocks

< 13" >	< 13" >	< 15" >
B	B	B
B	B	B
B	B	B
B	B	B
B	B	B
B	B	B
B	B	B Extra
B	B	B Extra
B	B	

3 ¼ Yards

4 ¼ Yards

Sashing
Back or Front

Betweens
Betweens
Vertical
Vertical
Vertical
Perimeter
Perimeter
Perimeter

(8) (8)

Perimeter

DOUBLE/QUEEN SIZE

Mattress . . . . .54" x 75"

. . . . .60" x 80"

Finished Quilt . . . . .88" x 104"

Blocks 20

Sashing size . . . . .4"

Borders . . . . .10"

FABRICS REQUIRED

Blocks (front) . . . . .7½ yds.

Sashing (front) . . . . .4¼ yds.

Borders . . . . .3½ yds.

Cornerstones (optional) . . . . .½ yd.

Back Totals . . . . .11 yds.

Blocks . . . . .3¼ yds.

Sashing . . . . .4¼ yds.

Borders . . . . .3½ yds.

Batting . . . . .90" x 108"

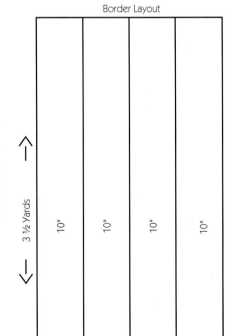

Border Layout

3 ½ Yards

10" 10" 10" 10"

Back of Blocks

< 13" > < 13" > < 15" >

B B B

3 ¼ Yards

4 ¼ Yards

Sashing
Back or Front

Betweens Betweens Vertical Vertical Vertical 2 Perimeter 2 Perimeter Perimeter

(8) (8)

Perimeter

CUTTING LAYOUT

KING SIZE

Mattress . . . . .76" x 80"
Finished Quilt . . . . .104" x 104"
Blocks 25
Sashing . . . . .4"
Borders . . . . .10"

FABRIC REQUIREMENTS

Blocks (front) . . . . .8½ yds.

Sashing (front) . . . . .5 yds.
Borders . . . . .3½ yds.
Cornerstones (optional) . . . . .½ yd.
Back Totals . . . . .12 yds.
  Blocks . . . . .3½ yds.
  Sashing . . . . .5 yds.
  Borders . . . . .3½ yds.
Batting King Size . . . . .120" x 120"

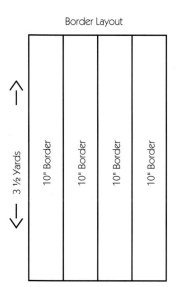

Border Layout

3 ½ Yards

10" Border / 10" Border / 10" Border / 10" Border

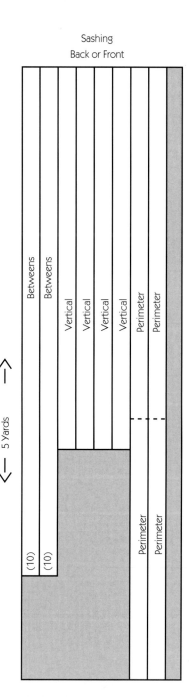

Sashing
Back or Front

5 Yards

Betweens / Betweens / Vertical / Vertical / Vertical / Vertical / Perimeter / Perimeter

Perimeter / Perimeter

(10) (10)

Back of Blocks

< 13" >

< 15" >

3 ½ Yards

B B B
B B B
B B B
B B B
B B B
B B B
B B B
B B B
B B B — Extra

Books
American Quilter's Society
P.O. Box 3290
Paducah, KY 42002-3290
1-800-626-5420

Magazines
The Creative Machine
The Open Chain Publishing, Inc.
P.O. Box 2634-B
Menlo Park, CA 94026
(415) 366-4440

Fabric Dyeing
Pro Chemical & Dye Inc.
P.O. Box 14
Somerset, MA 02726
1-800-2-BUY-DYE

Hancock's
PFD Fabrics (Kona Cotton)
3841 Hinkleville Road
Paducah, KY 42001
1-800-845-8723

Robert Kaufman Co., Inc.
(businesses only)
Pimatex (Prepared for Dyeing)
129 W 132nd Street
Los Angeles, CA 90061
1-800-877-2066

Testfabrics,Inc.
P.O. Box Drawer "O"
Middlessex, NJ 08846
(732) 469-6446

Mail Order Fabrics
G Street Fabrics
11854 Rockville Pike
Rockville, MD 20852
1-800-333-9191

Mary Jo's
401 Cox Rd.
Gastonia, NC 28054
1-800 Mary Jos

Notions
Clotilde, Inc. B3000
Louisiana, MO 63353
1-800-772-2891

Pictures in Quilts
Kensington Copy Center
3833 Plyers Mill Road
Kensington, MD 20895
(301) 933-6206

Quilting Designs
Beautiful Publications, LLC
13340 Harrison Street
Thornton, CO 80241-1403
(303) 452-3337

Threads
Web of Thread (catalog $3)
1410 Broadway
Paducah, KY 42001
1-800- 955-8185

BIBLIOGRAPHY

Birren, Faber. *Color Perception in Art*. West Chester, PA: Schiffer Publishing LTD, 1990.

_____. *Creative Color*. West Chester, PA: Schiffer Publishing LTD, 1987.

Buffington, Adriene. *Hand-Dyed Fabric Made Easy*. Bothell, WA: That Patchwork Place, 1996.

Byer, Jinny. *The Quilter's Album of Blocks and Borders*. EPM, 1980.

Johnston, Ann. *Dye Painting!* Paducah, KY: American Quilter's Society, 1992.

Spence, Kittie. *Quilt Designs from Indian Art*. Tucson, AZ: Mori Publications, 1982.

Struthers, Marilyn. *Curved Strip Piecing*. Winnipeg, Manitoba, Canada: PH Press, 1988.

ACKNOWLEDGMENTS

Thank you Hazel Carter for the use of your Virginia Star block design and Hari Walner for your continuous-line quilting pattern. Thank you Eleanor Burns for the term, "fussy cutting." Deep appreciation to Bernina of America and the New Home Sewing Machine Company for the use of loaner machines.

THANKS!

How great it is to have raised seven children who now have the all the writing, editing, and computer skills I needed to call upon to complete this book! Thanks! A note of sincere appreciate to my friend, Judy Lundberg, for sharing her expertise in the printing field, and to Jill Ruspi for her time spent reading and weeding out unnecessary words in this manuscript.

About the Author

An energetic person and passionate quilter, Lois Tornquist Smith enjoys taking her work in new directions as she explores challenging new techniques. Lois teaches the basic skills of quiltmaking as essential stepping stones for innovative and creative quilts. The goal of each quilt started, she stresses, is to finish. A teacher and judge certified by the National Quilting Association, Lois takes particular delight in watching beginning students thrill to quiltmaking.

In 1989 "Golden Memories of Christmas" was one of the first machine stitched quilts to take Best of Show at the Houston Quilt Festival. Her "Summertime Sampler" quilt won a ribbon at the AQS show and is now a part of the permanent collection of the Museum of the American Quilter's Society. Her quilts feature unique and innovative techniques and outstanding use of color.

Lois is a member of Uncommon Threads, a fiber art group, which displays works in and around the Washington, DC area.

Lois is married to Donovan A. Smith. They share their time between Rockville, Maryland, and a home on Chincoteague Island, Virginia. The Smiths have seven children and six grandchildren.

AQS BOOKS ON QUILTS

This is only a partial listing of the books on quilts that are available from the American Quilter's Society. AQS books are known the world over f[or] their timely topics, clear writing, beautiful color photographs, and accurate illustrations and patterns. Most of the following books are available fro[m] your local bookseller, quilt shop, or public library. If you are unable to locate certain titles in your area, you may order by mail from the AMERICA[N] QUILTER'S SOCIETY, P.O. Box 3290, Paducah, KY 42002-3290. Customers with Visa or MasterCard may phone in orders from 7:00–5:00 CS[T] Monday–Friday, Toll Free 1-800-626-5420. Add $2.00 for postage for the first book ordered and $0.40 for each additional book. Include item numbe[r,] title, and price when ordering. Allow 14 to 21 days for delivery.